The Idiom of Love

The Idiom of Love

Love Poetry from the Early Sonnets to the Seventeenth Century

Judy Sproxton

Duckworth

First published in 2000 by
Gerald Duckworth & Co. Ltd.
61 Frith Street, London W1V 5TA
Tel: 0207 434 4242
Fax: 0207 434 4420
Email: enquiries@duckworth-publishers.co.uk

A CIP catalogue record for this title is available from the British Library.

ISBN 0 7156 2826 7

Typeset by Derek Doyle & Associates, Liverpool
Printed in Great Britain by
Redwood Books Ltd, Trowbridge

Contents

Preface

Many people have helped in the realisation of this book. My great thanks are due to Robin Baird-Smith, who commissioned it and whose interest, patience and confidence sustained me over an extremely busy time, when both teaching and writing claimed precedence. I should also like to thank him for introducing me to Paul Oppenheimer. Paul Oppenheimer's book, *The Birth of the Modern Mind*, led me to focus on the origins of the tensions in the love poetry of Western Europe. The insight his scholarship provided enabled me to interpret the lyric poetry which emerged from the first compositions for silent reading, as a dialogue with the self. With his permission I have drawn on his translations of the sonnets of Giacomo da Lentino. As well as for his scholarship, I am grateful for his interest in my work and the comments on my ideas which he has generously offered.

Other friends and colleagues have also helped me with support and invigorating discussion. My husband Nick has allowed himself to be enticed by the subject of this book almost as often s I have demanded that he should. Richard Parish read and discussed much of my work in its early stages. Nicholas Hammond and Jonathan Finlay have also offered valuable comment. Peter Ricketts kindly gave me a copy of his inaugural lecture, 'A Fine Romance', from which I have with his permission taken his translation of a section of a text by Bernart de Ventadorn. I am also grateful to Philip Ford and Gillian Jondorf, editors of *Women's Writing in the Renaissance*

(Cambridge 1999) for giving me permission to reproduce a substantial part of my paper on Louise Labé. The students of 'Ethos and Expression' which I taught at Birmingham were tremendously helpful in their response. To be in contact with young alert minds is a constant stimulus. This is why I have dedicated this book to my children, who never cease to surprise me.

A last acknowledgement must be given to my editor at Duckworth, Martin Rynja, who has been consistently enthusiastic and helpful.

My next acknowledgement will be of a different kind. I acknowledge that my book may be found selective. It is true that I have limited my comments to a very narrow area in the literature of Western Europe. However, there is no canon for love poetry at any stage. The period from which I have made my selection is unique in that it witnessed a confrontation with the self, informed by silent reading. Writers in this period had a spiritual consciousness promoted by the ubiquitous presence of faith. The choice of the theme of love was one that highlighted the passionate vulnerability of humanity. Such a heady mixture made for a fertile nourishment of ironies and contradictions, which formed the crux of their poetry.

The richness differs from the more monochrome presentation of love often found elsewhere. The Song of Solomon in the Old Testament burgeons with expressions of longing and images of intimacy, but as A.S. Byatt points out in her introduction to the Canongate edition (1998), the Fathers of the Church rationalised the Song to present a text which they claimed to speak of love of the incarnate Word. The result of what A.S. Byatt terms their 'ingenuity and resourceful reconstructions and deconstructions' leave the reader baffled. We do not find here a genuine fusion of the consciousness of passion and of God. Rather, the latter serves to annihilate the former.

Leaping to a modern era, various attempts have been made to offer a scientific explanation of love. Recently researchers in an Italian University identified a biochemical protein which they claimed indicated whether someone had 'really' fallen in love. They claimed to have found a common pattern of brain cells similar to that of people suffering an obsessive, compulsive disorder. The blood of such people apparently shows a forty per cent loss of a protein which helps serotonin, a neurotransmitter, to travel from one nerve cell to another. The researchers decided that the initial stage of falling in love had the same effect as development of a manic obsession with cleaning. Both the scholastic and scientific approach to love are self-evidently reductive. Their claim to be objective removes the essential factor, which alone can make any approach to love plausible.

One particular omission in my discussion might be found unacceptable: I have not referred to bawdy poetry. There is of course much scurrilous rhyme from the Middle Ages onward, but again, this type of verse excludes any genuine debate in the mind of writer or reader. It is a moral anaesthetic. Such verse demeans love, reducing it to a physical indulgence which detracts from the respect owed by definition to any human preoccupation. The *Idiom of Love* seeks to identify the nobility in an attempt to make a work of art out of the paradox of human experience – much as we might feel shamed by our distressing propensity to passionate response to create poetry from it and read this poetry, give it some kind of reason for being.

Stratford-upon-Avon
December 1999

For
Oliver, Jessica and Sam

Introduction

The Scholars

Bald heads forgetful of their sins,
Old, learned, respectable bald heads
Edit and annotate the lines
That young men, tossing on their beds,
Rhymed out in love's despair
To flatter beauty's ignorant ear.

All shuffle there; all cough in ink;
All wear the carpet with their shoes;
All think what other people think;
All know the man their neighbour knows.
Lord, what would they say
Did their Catullus walk that way?

W. B. Yeats

In this poem, Yeats asserts a fundamental incompatibility between love poetry and scholarship. It would indeed be indefensible to write about love poetry in such a lifeless way as to distance the poetry from a reader. However, the aim of this book is not to dissect, but to revitalise the love poetry it discusses. I have sought to bring another dimension to the reading of certain poems by suggesting the main preoccupations of their writers. An understanding of these should, I hope, make the poems clearer, and their effect greater. I hope that the affection which has lasted over the years for many of the poems discussed in this book, will be increased by a wider appreciation of the poets' experience of writing them. It is more than possible that *ignorance* of the climate of the writer's time, and of his personal perspective, will confuse the reader's response and create a gulf between him and what he reads.

Today writing a poem is most often seen as a highly personal venture. But before the invention of printing, literacy was the prerogative of the Church alone. The Church owned the manuscripts which had survived from ancient Greece and Rome. It effectively eliminated access to such works and absorbed into its own teaching all knowledge and intellectual energy. For a mentality which conceived creation in terms of an exclusive hierarchy, with God – that is to say, the Church at its head, the individual was an irrelevant nonentity.

This book begins where self-awareness became, for the first time since classical antiquity, a factor in the mind of writer and reader. The twelfth century saw the dawn of the modern conception of self-consciousness, and of the expression of individual experience. Such a dimension contrasted strongly with the monolithic presence of the Roman Catholic Church. It implied an essential insecurity and vulnerability.

Writing poetry in the Middle Ages involved awareness of many factors. The poet needed to justify such writing; what was its value, if any? He would also be conscious of the peril of his spiritual identity, of the action of writing in the sight of God. The highly personal theme of love took him away from the teaching of the Church, which, since the start of the Crusades, promoted celibacy. Was such a theme simply an indication of madness?

Introduction

The concepts of writing, of love, of the individual's relationship with God were understood differently throughout the Middle Ages, the Renaissance and the post-Renaissance period. It would be an invidious task, involving much coughing in ink, to try and chart the development of the kaleidoscopic perspectives resulting from the interplay of these notions. In the course of this book, it will become clear that writing poetry involved more than the recording of an isolated, personal sentiment. But it would be a grave mistake to allow the individual writer to be engulfed in the morass of the cultural context. The particular mark of the individual writer is an invaluable feature, and indeed indicates the courage with which certain writers rose to the challenge of creating an identity beyond the bounds which their surrounding culture sought to impose.

This high degree of inventiveness creates the theme for this book: the *idiom* of love. The word 'idiom' indicates something personal and private, peculiar and separate. It also suggests a form of language which has a peculiar phraseology. Looking at various writers who have chosen love as their theme, one is aware that each conceives and expresses love in an impressively peculiar way. Such diversity of interpretation calls into question any attempt to standardise the term 'love'. We find that questions of faith, of identity, of confrontation with the self are drawn into the individual writer's response to this theme as well as the portrayal of a specific relationship. The references in this poetry differ so widely that, to the modern reader, its perspective is often baffling, yet always ultimately stimulating.

I have aimed throughout to distinguish between one writer and another by drawing attention to the very singularity of each. This is not to say that such poets were endeavouring to cut themselves off from tradition, or from the fashion of their age. But in order to make an impact on his reader, or on himself, the writer was drawn to find a specific approach to his subject which would arouse or express attention to the singularity of his problem. Love implies an overwhelming experience of the mind, over which the intellect initially seems to have no control. It is at this point that despair calls on the young man of Yeats's poem to rhyme out his love: not only to 'flatter beauty's ignorant ear', but to create something memorable from the scattered elements of his personal quandary.

1

Courtly Love and Conscious Love

The earliest examples of love poetry in the vernacular appeared in thirteenth-century Europe. Most famously the songs of the troubadours of southern France presented tales of love for entertainment in the court of the aristocracy. The troubadours themselves were of disparate origin. Often they were clerics who wanted to be free from monastic life, or whose order had fallen on hard times. Such men sought patronage from the courts. Other troubadours may well have had a more genteel origin and were themselves knights or petty nobility. Nor were their songs confined to the theme of love; some were scurrilous or satirical. In Northern France, for example, the *chanson de geste* developed, which recounted epic battles and the noble pursuit of warfare. The tradition of *fin amor*, or courtly love, however, is exclusively identifiable in the songs of the troubadours of the south. This presentation of love is highly stylised and, even today, the term 'courtly love' typifies in the minds of many people an approach to love celebrated in the Middle Ages. C. S. Lewis saw in it the origin of the etiquette of love which prevails in the twentieth century, and which marks out relationships between the sexes from that found in African or Eastern countries (*The Allegory of Love*).

The poetry of the troubadours was designed for performance in

15

a specific social setting. Its predictability and repetitiveness also suggest the static nature of the society for which it was intended. The language and phraseology, the situations and the relationships recounted in the songs, all echo one another. The love described in the *canzo* of the troubadour is presented by the singer as his own tale; he is both performer and persona. The love of which he sings is directed towards a lady of high birth. She is beautiful and has elevated moral qualities. She is usually married to someone of high rank, often absent. The troubadour addresses her as *midons*, my Lord, which implies that she has in his eyes taken on the feudal power of her husband. This situation in some ways reflects genuine features of feudal society, where the lord of the manor was often away hunting, or fighting in a crusade.

However, insistence on the supremacy of a woman was not an accepted feature of feudal society, since it was so much at odds with the view of the Church. Christian theology of the period held a misogynist view of women, since women were associated with Eve's temptation of Adam. Sexual relations were held by Thomas Aquinas, who wrote the definitive theology of the medieval Church, to be sinful, unless pursued exclusively for the purpose of creating children. The cult of the Virgin Mary honoured exclusively her divine motherhood. One can assume, then, that the love pattern which was expressed by the troubadours in their songs of courtly love was nurtured to some degree by a collective fantasy. Such fantasy, however, provides its own insight into a society. The troubadours' song, despite its incompatibility with the social and theological norm, was rigorous in its consistency with itself; the pattern never varies. In every *canzo* the poet / persona sees the lady and falls in love. She remains haughty and aloof, indifferent to his presence or his pleas. Because of her high rank and, more often than not, her married status, she is inaccessible. This barrier would appear to inspire the lover, who begs her for a token of some kind to indicate response, however minimal. Another movement derives from the danger in which the poet / persona has allegedly placed himself through his attentions to the lady, since she is surrounded by her husband's servants. This situation is presented in the song as a challenge, since only through patience, and suppression of his distress, can he hope to obtain some recognition from her. In this way, his love demands a repression of self. Just as the situation in the troubadour's poem is stereotypical, so is the poet / persona's presentation of himself. In fact, although nominally the poet sings of the lady, the poem focuses principally on the trials of the lover. (In some rare cases, the persona is a female lover; there were some female courtly love poets, though not many.) Banished from the beloved by physical barriers as well as by her hostility, or pretence of rejection, the poet's only residual subject matter is his state of mind which is shown to veer between hope and despair. It is implied that he must bear this ordeal if he is to be worthy of his lady. However, although the poetry purports to tell of the poet's state of mind, it is not introspective. It merely repeats a series of disjointed emotions which illustrate the lack of control the human mind has over itself.

The pattern of all the troubadours' songs recognises a certain ethos. Although the status of the lady in the song runs counter to the official misogyny of the Middle Ages, the state of mind attributed by the poet / persona to himself is consistent with the state of subservience promoted in the period by both Church and feudal system. The poet describes himself as essentially centreless, motivated only by his adoration of the lady. The theology of the Middle Ages stated that the distance from God caused by original sin had

17

left man irrational. The 'naturalness' described by Aristotle had been adopted by the Church, and was seen to be intransigent, relegating the individual to a worthless nonentity; St Augustine's assertion in the early 400s A. D., of the acceptability of faith to God was the conceivable means by which this inevitable division might be breached. But that in itself implied subservience and suspicion of the workings of the human mind. The order of the universe, established by divine Reason and reflected in the teachings of the Church, was seen as a circumscription to all epistemology. In other words, this imposed the grammar for understanding everything. The individual had no role other than to respect the supremacy of divine Reason, embodied in the Church, and to humble himself before it. He could attain an identity only through adherence to a worthy institution, for this adherence would make him part of that institution. In this respect, the Church and feudal society itself were all-powerful. The ethos of the troubadour poetry reflects the vacuity of the individual, as he was regarded then. Emotions are personified in the songs, and presented as typical features of a passive, powerless being. There is no self-consciousness in these poems. The medieval idea of a timeless structure established by God and reflected in the social hierarchy is echoed in the lyrics of the troubadours. The scornful, dismissive lady of the troubadour poem reflects a remote God, who is assuaged only by humility and prayer. Most importantly, whoever seeks to win acknowledgement from this powerful being must look beyond himself, dismissing his own questions and accepting his own insignificance.

I have chosen a poem by Bernart de Ventadorn (Lazar edition) to illustrate these typical features of the troubadour poem. It begins by contrasting the inactivity of the poet before he fell in

love, with his present obsession. He is now compelled to sing of
his passion:

> *Lonc tems a qu'eu no chantei mai*
> *ni saubi far chaptenemen*
> *Ara no tema ploya ni ven,*
>   *tan sui entratz en cossire*
>   *com pogues bos motz assire*
>   *en est so c'ai apedit.*
> *Sitot no.m vei flor ni folha,*
> *melhs me vai c'al tems florit,*
> *car l'amors qu'eu plus volh, me vol.*

It is a long time since I ceased to sing / and since I could behave in
a fitting manner. / Now I fear neither rain nor wind / so preoccupied am I by the thought / of how I might set fine words to / the
melody I have composed. / Although I see neither flower nor leaf it
goes better with me than in the spring / for the love which I most
desire, desires me.

The concept of singing his love song and 'behaving in a fitting
manner' are linked here; it is as if the lover only recognises that he
exists through his response to the lady. He boasts of his indifference
to the wind and rain, and also to the absence of spring, since his sole
preoccupation is with love. The statement *'l'amors qu'eu plus volh,
me vol'* suggests a reciprocal effect; this state of mind is self-engen-
dering, and excludes all else. In the following stanza, he triumphantly
proclaims the well-being that his love has brought him:

> *E s'eu anc fui bos sofrire,*
> *ara me tenh per garit,*
> *qu'e re no sen mal que.me dolha.*

19

And if I had to suffer much formerly, / I hold myself to be cured now / for in no way do I feel any pain which makes me suffer.

The state of being in love with his lady is shown as the absolute joy. It immures him from all distress, and restores him beyond recognition.

In the Middle Ages, family ties and friendship were held to be paramount factors in identity and allegiance. The troubadour in this song makes a point of putting such obligations second to his devotion to his lady. He wishes to keep his love for her secret, even from them as well as from all others who might claim his allegiance.

> *El mon tan bon amic non ai,*
> *fraire ni cozi ni paren,*
> *que, si.m vai mo joi enqueren,*
> *qu'ins e mo cor no.l n'azire,*
> *e s'eu m'en volh escondire.*

In all the world, I do not have such a good friend, / brother, cousin or relation / whom I do not hate with all my heart, / if he goes prying into the source of my joy.

The singer makes it clear that he does not ask much; merely from a 'kind expression' which she might bestow on him when the occasion permits, he ' has so much joy that I lose all my senses'. However, his fantasies do not stop here. Shortly after rhapsodising about the joy her 'kind expression' inspires, he begins to hypothesise other delights, such as being allowed to see her undress in a private place. Musing on the likelihood that this might not happen, he starts to get angry:

1. Courtly Love and Conscious Love

Si no.m aizis lai on ilh jai
si qu'eu remir son bel cors gen,
doncs, per que m'a faih de nien?
Ai las! Com mor de dezire!
Vol me doncs midons aucire,
car l'am? O que lh'ai falhit?

If she does not admit me to where she lies / so that I may feast my eyes on her fine, noble body /, why did she raise me out of nothing? Alas! How I die from desire! Does my lady wish to kill me / since I love her? Or what have I done to her?

Rapidly, however, he regains his control and reverts to his former position of total acquiescence.

mas ilh s'en prend' esgardamen
qu'eu non ai d'alire pessamen
mas com li fos bos sevire.

but let her give due regard to the fact that I have no other thought / than to be her servant.

The poem ends with the statement that his passion for the lady alone has enabled him to sing, and for this he thanks her.

This song starts with the idea of song: love has inspired the troubadour to sing. His passion makes little progress. It veers from total joy at the slightest thing to abject despair at the lack of opportunity granted him. Ultimately, his only success would appear to lie in his readiness to submit himself absolutely to his lady's will. And the only fruit of this convoluted tale is the song itself: the song ends with idea of the song as fulfilment in itself.

21

The similar pattern of the troubadour songs makes one thing clear; they were composed to respond to a particular taste. Like the modern pop song, their value lay in the degree to which they express a collective fantasy, or perhaps serve to create one.

However, the troubadour song was not the only form of love lyric to appear in the early Middle Ages, although it took root and was popular for a very long time. In the court of Frederick II of Sicily around the beginning of the thirteenth century, the first sonnets were written. Thanks to the work of Paul Oppenheimer (*The Birth of the Modern Mind*, Oxford, 1989), the importance of this form has been made clear. The fundamental difference between the sonnet and the troubadour song was that the sonnet was written not to be sung but to be read silently. The form of the sonnet, in fourteen lines, did not correspond to any medieval musical score. The octave was adopted from the Sicilian peasant song; the sestet, which extends and completes the sonnet, was added by a lawyer at Frederick's court, Giacomo da Lentino. This form was fundamentally different form the lengthy, rambling strophes of the courtly love lyric, since within its brief space it provided the scope for an individual writer to recount and respond to his own experience. The sonnet introduced an individual experience of personal reality and a new self-consciousness, rather than echoing the hollow pomp of the court with remote, sugary illusion. Such a dimension had never entered the troubadours' song. The poet / persona of this song denigrated his individuality and showed it to be subsumed by total submission and self-effacement. The sonnet which appeared in the court of Frederick II, revived for the first time since the classical literature of Greece and Rome the personal, moral element in literature in which an individual is shown to be confronted by the immediate challenges of his own being and by his involvement with others. The Church's suppression of Greek and Roman literature had inevitably led to the spread of allegory, which dictated that meaning was only to be found through analogy with the teaching of the Church. This influence led human beings to rely exclusively on the Church for an explanation of existence. There was no room for introspection nor self-questioning. The rigorous structure of Thomist Aristotelianism meant that all was explained and explicable. Anything beyond this explanation simply was considered not to exist at all. To dwell on the fragmentary experience of the individual was thus useless. However, in the court of Frederick II, a way of thinking and writing began to flourish which anticipated the Renaissance in its emphasis on the experience of the individual and his response to it. The sonnet bears testament to this. It is important to remember that the sonnet was a new experience for the recipient as well as for the writer. Whereas the troubadours had devised their poetry as song, the earliest sonnets were not set to music, as many people still assume. The first musical settings of sonnets date from 1470. The early sonnets were written to be read silently, or at most to a few people.

The development of the sonnet indicates a way of thinking and writing which anticipated the Renaissance in its emphasis on the experience of the individual and his response to it. The climate of the court of Frederick II encouraged this development. Frederick lived from 1196 until 1250. His own personality did much to dynamise the life of his court. Sicily was a vibrant place, at the crossroads of many cultures, both from the east and from the west of Europe. Frederick was culturally ambitious and had a travelling theatre which roamed the countryside presenting astonishing spectacles to the people. These were primarily designed as a celebration of Frederick's power and glory. Apart from his egocentric roadshow, Frederick contributed personally to the cultural achievement of his court. He compiled a book called *De arte venandi cum avibus*, an illustrated treatise on hunting with birds. This text was exceptional for its time, since its material derived from direct experience. Frederick declared that his aim in the book was 'to present things as they are'. This aim was in total contrast to the spirit of the medieval Church, which insisted on the presentation of all data according to Aristotelian 'naturalness', which constituted a rigorous order of supremacy and distanced man from God. From the Church's viewpoint, the senses were deceptive, and so, to bear any relation to truth, all themes must be presented in terms of their affinity with God or with Biblical texts. Bestiaries compiled by monks contained illustrated accounts of animals re-enacting episodes from the Old and New Testaments. Frederick II was consciously opposed to such fallacies. He declaimed that we should accept as truth that which is found by the force of reason and by nature. Consequently, his book on hunting with birds contained illustrations taken from what the artist experienced and observed.

Frederick was certainly at odds with the Church in many ways. In 1221, he founded the university of Naples which stood as a direct challenge to the papal university of Bologna. The university of Naples was designed for the formation of lawyers, and Giacomo da Lentino was certainly a visitor there. In this university Platonic philosophy was taught, based on the Platonic dialogues. It was hardly surprising that Frederick was excommunicated three times. It was equally unsurprising that the sonnet should have emerged from such a vibrant cultural context.

1. Courtly Love and Conscious Love

The sonnet combines, in the short space of fourteen lines, both past and present. The present experience of the writer is presented in the first eight lines, as a difficulty in which he is currently involved. Through a sudden change of perspective in the concluding sestet, another dimension is added: that of the writer's reflection on his experience. The pattern of the sonnet promotes reflection. Its content is not simply presented: it is also resolved, in a very particular way, which only the writer himself could achieve. The momentum of the sonnet came from the writer's insistence on some kind of resolution. Unlike the troubadours' song, it was not compiled to suit the taste of an audience, formed by habit. It spoke of emotion confronted and, in some highly personal way, resolved. Through the creation of a sonnet from his own depiction of emotional conflict, the writer was able at the same time to draw on the personal response of his reader. It was an essentially introspective, intimate way of writing.

Poetry written to be silently read and to consider, alone or almost alone, involved a complexity which the troubadours' song could not approach. Designed for performance, the troubadours' lyric was compiled to accompany music, and must not detract from it. Therefore its substance was often thin. Drawn out on a narrative line, it had little room for complex images or convoluted emotions, designed to be experienced all at the same time. The sonnet, on the other hand, was able to penetrate into the inner recesses of the psyche. A new imaginative richness developed through the sonnet, in which concrete images replaced allegorical personification and referred to subconscious realities, of which writer and reader could be aware only in their personal lives. The many layers of the sonnet could appeal both emotively and intellectually. Above all, the sonnet was a medium for the expression of essential contradiction in human experience, where self-awareness compelled acknowledgement of the paradox of conflicting emotions. The sonnet was able to express these emotions, and also to add a further dimension: the resolution of their co-existence through the poet's intellectual grasp of his dilemma. He could create conceits, comparisons, ironies, all of which contributed to the illumination of self-knowledge amidst the presence of another perspective of truth. Such a creative struggle had not been witnessed in European literature since the enforced banishment of Homer, Sophocles and Catullus.

The first known sonnets written in the court of Frederick II, provide examples of the striking creativity they engendered. Giacomo da Lentino took love as his theme. But unlike the troubadours, he did not present love in a setting in which the lover is physically banished from his lady, and has to grovel to gain access to her and withstand the threat of protective servants loyal to her husband. In Giacomo's sonnets, the struggle is within the heart of the lover himself. He writes of love as a highly individual experience, using novel imagery to convey its effect.

Giacomo's Sonnet XI illustrates the reflexivity made possible by the sonnet form. Although its reference to the sickness of love and the apparent indifference of his beloved are themes found in the troubadours' songs, the sonnet is clearly different in form and in content from them. It is not addressed to an audience. It suggests the gnawing presence of the problems of love in the poet's mind. In the 'turn' of the sestet, the poet considers his plight from another perspective: this love is part of the experience of being human. It links him with others. The mind is bound to wrestle with the problem of love, as an acknowledgement of humanity.

1. Courtly Love and Conscious Love

Molti amadori la lor malatia
portano in core, che'm vista nom pare;
ed io nom posso, sì celar la mia
ch'ella nom paia per lo mio penare;

peró che son sotto altrui segnoria
né di meve non ó neiente a fare,
se non quanto madonna mia voria,
ch'ella mi pote morte e vita dare,

Su' èlo core, e suo sono tutto quanto,
e chi non á comsiglio da suo core,
non vive imfra la gente como deve.

Cád io nom sono mio né più nè tanto
se non quanto madonna è de mi fore,
ed un poco di spirito ch'è 'n meve.

So many lovers carry their love-disease /
Inside their heart where it cannot be seen,
But I cannot conceal my fierce unease
So that it does not glimmer through my pain;

I'm under just one woman's haughty eye,
She neither stirs nor does a thing in truth –
Unless my lady make me some reply,
Because she can pronounce my life or death.

My heart is hers, me too – all, all for her –
And he who fails to listen to his heart
Can't live with people as he should, or share

I suffer thus: am neither here nor there,
Unless my lady guides me, though apart,
Unless my bit of spirit guides me, here.

Sonnet IX uses metaphors drawn from nature, both to demonstrate the basic qualities of love, and to suggest the challenge it
presents to the human mind:

Lo giglio quand'è colto tost'è passo
la poi la sua natura lui no è giunta
ed io, dacunque son partuto un passo
da voi, mia donna, dolemi ogni giunta:

perché d'amare ogni amadore passo
in tante alteze lo mio core giunta;
così mi fere Amor, lavunque passo,
com 'aghila quand'a la caccia è giunta.

Oi lasso me, che nato fui in tal punto
s'unque no amasse se non voi, Chiú – gente!
Questo saccio, madonna, da mia parte:

in prima che vi vidi ne fui punto,
serviivi ed inoraivi a tutta gente;
da voi, bella, lo mio core non parte.

Once cut, the lily fades, and very fast –
Once cheated, naturally of its basic nature.
So I: deprived of you, I seem to fast
And fade with pains of every possible nature.

1. Courtly Love and Conscious Love

For love like mine secures itself, too fast,
To heights unknown to hearts of a weaker nature,
So too, my love impales me, far too fast,
An eagle swooping, ravaging by nature.

How hopeless I would be, born to this fate,
If I loved someone else – not you, the best!
This knowledge, Lady, is certain on my part:

At once, on seeing you, I knew my fate –
To serve and praise you everywhere as best.
From you, my love, my heart can never part.

This sonnet, like many in Giacomo's early work, uses 'tag' words rather than rhymes; these are meant to act as a focus for play on words, since the same word is often given a different meaning in the text. The principal images in this sonnet are drawn from nature: the lover compares himself to a lily which fades once its stem is cut. A similar fate befalls the lover, once deprived of his beloved. In the second stanza he berates himself for aspiring too high and for risking himself too quickly; the images of height and risk are identified by the description of love as an eagle, whose nature is to swoop and ravage. The 'turn' of the sonnet comes in the sestet, where there are no images, but in which the lover concludes that his plight would truly be hopeless, if he had not chosen this lady to be his love. Her worth surpasses all the danger and deprivation that loving her entails. The sonnet is markedly different from the troubadours' usual song, principally through its stance. Initially the lover is described reflecting on the perils of his state of mind. In the sestet, he returns openly to his beloved and addresses her. The lover is no longer in a world apart from his beloved, as in the courtly love poems. He speaks to her directly.

Another early sonnet by Giacomo illustrates the impact of his choice of imagery. In this sonnet, he likens the way in which love passes into the heart with light passing through glass. Since glass, particularly lenses, was such a rarity at this time, developing in Venice before spreading slowly throughout Europe, such a simile would undoubtedly be striking. He also refers to the reflective properties of the glass mirror, which he uses to indicate the double edge of love; if it is reciprocated it changes utterly:

Sí come il sol, che manda la sua spera
e passa per lo vetro e no lo parte.
e l'altro vetro che le donne spera,
che passa gli occhi e va da l'altra parte,

cosí l'Amore fera là ove spera
e mandavi lo dardo da sua parte:
fere in tal loco che l'omo non spera,
e passa gli occhi e lo core diparte.

Lo dardo de l'Amore, là ove giunge,
da poi che dà feruta sí s'aprende
di foco, ch'arde dentro e fuor non pare;

e li due cori insemola li giunge:
de l'arte de l'Amore sí gli aprende,
e face l'uno e l'altro d'amor pare.
Just as the sun can spear right through the face

1. *Courtly Love and Conscious Love*

Of any glass and no one seems to mind,
And like the glass that spears a woman's face
Straight through her eyes and climbs into her mind –

Just so true love can manage to deface
Wherever it wishes, shooting time out of mind
The pang whose pain you feel you cannot face,
To send you, through your eyes, out of your mind.

The pain of love, precisely where you feel it,
And once the pain begins, transforms itself
To fire, shrewd and cold, that none can see.

But if the fire's doubled, by two who feel it,
The power to love once more transforms itself,
Inspiring both with love that both can see.

The 'turn' of this sonnet depends on the essential feature of change; just as fire is used to make glass, response can create something substantial between two lovers.

One last sonnet (XVIII) serves to illustrate the richness of Giacomo's poetry. Here the text is extended by reference to mythology; Giacomo cites the basilisk, the dying swan and the peacock as examples of paradox in which beauty and awareness of imminent death co-exist. In the sestet, he declares how his love, like these legendary beasts, contains the same paradoxical elements:

Lo basalisco a lo speccio lucente
traggi a morire con isbaldimento:

The Idiom of Love .

lo cesne canta piú gioiosamente
quand'è piú presso a lo so finimento;

lo paon turba, quando è piú gaudente,
poi ch'a suoi piedi fa riguardamento;
l'augel fenise s'arde verament
per ritornare in novo nascimento:

In tal nature eo sentom'abenuto,
ch'allegro vado a more a le belleze
e'nforzo il canto presso a lo fenire,

e stando gaio torno dismaruto,
e ardendo in foco invoco in allegreze
per voi, Piú-gente, e cui spero redire.

The basilisk before a lucid mirror
Surrenders to death in joyful agony;
The swan keeps singing with a joyful horror
When overwhelmed by its mortality;

The peacock, at its height of brilliant plumes,
Shivers in horror on glancing at its feet;
The phoenix bird consumes itself in flames
Completely to return, reborn, complete.

I feel myself becoming this sort of creature –
Happy to meet my death before great beauty
And pushing my song to glory at its last turn.

1. Courtly Love and Conscious Love

And right in the midst of joy feeling great torture,
And burning in flames, renewing my happy duty
To you – so fine – to whom I would return.

This exotic sonnet extends through its metaphorical connotations the richness of individual experience. The poet is no longer the self-effacing coward who appears in many courtly love poems; he has a greatness, implied through links with legendary beauty and courage. He also possesses a ravaging self-awareness, so that even his most intense delights are coloured by his sense of inadequacy and the imminence of death.

The idiom of love when expressed in the sonnet is no longer a fatuous device for predictable entertainment, as in the songs of the troubadours. It speaks of the inner self of both writer and reader.

2

Petrarch's Sonnets
The Idiom of Imperfection

Although Petrarch is remembered today as a poet, he was known in his own time as a moral philosopher. The vivid way in which Petrarch's sonnets portray the intensity and anguish of love is seminal and has formed the basis of the language of love since he first wrote. However, it is enlightening to look at this poetry with an awareness of his identity as a moral philosopher, since, seen from this perspective, his understanding of the effect of love becomes clearer.

Throughout his life Petrarch campaigned to rid the Church of corruption. In the early fourteenth century, because of secular power struggles within Rome, the papacy was transferred to Avignon. Petrarch strove for its return to Rome. He wrote several treatises in Latin on moral themes, such as an account of the lives of illustrious men, and definitions of the cardinal virtues. Petrarch was a scholar, musician, diplomat, and horticulturalist. Born in Arezzo in 1304, Petrarch was also an early humanist; he respected the value of texts written by the ancient Greeks and Romans. His contact with the Church allowed him access to ancient texts, which were all in the possession of monastic libraries. The Church sought to incorporate some of these into its own teaching, insisting that texts could have value only when absorbed into the corpus of the wisdom of the Church. In this way, it was hoped to remove all hint of challenge to the Church's claim to have exclusive insight into absolute truth.

However, Petrarch's independent reading gave him a respect for the value of individual experience. The orthodox theology of the fourteenth-century Church was a Christianised version of Aristotle's claim that nature disclosed the principle of the structure of creation: creation revealed a rational hierarchy. The assumption of divine logic presupposed an intrinsic account of all aspects of creation, which, sufficient in its own terms, inevitably excluded the experience of an individual. Petrarch, however, was drawn to the perspective of individual experience. He read widely amongst ancient writers, particularly Cicero, for a discussion of the importance of moral values in society, and the degree to which the individual was challenged to contribute to the social good. However, the writer by whom he was most influenced was St Augustine, a Church Father of the fifth century. Augustine had emphasised in his writing the importance of personal experience in the search for a full understanding of his existence from the perspective of faith. By exposing the devastating fallibility of his life, he thought to find the contrasting glory of God. His *Confessions* recount the susceptibility of youth to passions of the flesh. His detailed and exhaustive account of his helpless vulnerability was the foundation of his sense of man's need of God. Left to his own devices, Augustine concluded, man inevitably turned towards sin. The grace of God alone could deliver him from the imperfection of his condition. In his seminal work *The City of God* Augustine speaks of two perspectives, the worldly and the divine. To attain an appreciation of the divine, the worldly must first be recognised for all its false allure. Petrarch learned from Augustine that a reorientation of emotion and will can only proceed from consciousness of personal experience. Such a consciousness revealed the essential polarity between human weakness, and God's power. This insight made more sense to Petrarch than the insistence of the orthodox Thomist Aristotelian theology which derived intellectual and impersonal metaphysical truths from the apparent laws of creation, and thus presented a reductive and exclusive account of creation. This account condemned the criteria of the individual to irrelevancy. Mankind must be aware of humanity's distance from God, on whom alone depended salvation.

Petrarch's personal poetry, the *Canzoniere*, was written in Italian. In many circles, especially the Church, the vernacular was not considered appropriate at the time for writing of an elevated nature. However, Petrarch revised and polished the *Canzoniere* throughout his lifetime, and clearly valued it. This collection includes his three hundred and seventeen love sonnets, but also other reflective lyrics, some making particular reference to his religious faith. The immediacy and the highly charged impact of these poems owe much to the relative spontaneity of the vernacular. The fame of Petrarch's love sonnets has outlived his other writing. However, the importance of retaining a consciousness of the impact of personal experience, which he drew from Augustine, might well have had a substantial effect on the *Canzoniere*.

The sonnets of the *Canzoniere* basically recount one relationship. They do not constitute a narrative text telling a story in episodes as do many of the ballads of the troubadours. The theme is of love for a woman who is given the name Laura. Little is learned about Laura in the three hundred and sixty-six poems of the sequence. Indeed, her very existence was questioned by Petrarch's friend Giacomo Colonna. What emerges clearly is that Petrarch wished to recreate through his writing the intensity of this love, and perhaps his love of Laura, which he primarily conveys through his choice of images. The striking physicality of Petrarch's images etches on the reader's mind the experience of which he writes. The account of the state of being in love forms the substance of the *Canzoniere*. Petrarch's poems about Laura are usually viewed biographically by critics. Yet, since he fathered two illegitimate children, a son in 1337 and a daughter in 1343, the passion for Laura recorded in his poems was clearly not exclusive. It is possible that Petrarch wished, in fact, to write about the state of being in love itself, and that the figure of Laura formed a focus for this account.

Petrarch took care, when preparing his poems for publication, to set them in a context of moral challenge. The introductory sonnet, presumably composed later than the bulk of the poems, speaks of the distance that he now feels from the amorous state of mind, which retrospectively fills him with shame.

> *Voi ch'ascoltate in rime sparse il suono*
> *di quei sospiri ond'io nudriva 'l core*
> *in sul mio primo giovenile errore*
> *quand'era in parte altr'uom da quel ch'i'sono:*
>
> *del vario stile in ch'io piango et ragiono,*
> *fra le vane speranze e 'l van dolore,*
> *ove sia chi per prova intenda amore,*
> *spero trovar pietà non che perdono.*

2. Petrarch's Sonnets

Ma ben veggio or si come al popol tutto
favola fui gran tempo, onde sovente
di me medesmo meco mi vegogno;

e del mio vaneggiar vergogna é'l frutto
e'l pentersi, é'l conoscer chiaramente
che quanto piace al mondo ebreve sogno.

You who hear in scattered rhymes the sound of those sighs on which I fed my heart in the time of my first youthful error, when I was in part another man from the one I am now:

for the varied style in which I speak and lament, between vain hopes and vain sorrow, wherever there is someone who understands love from experience I hope to find not only pardon, but also pity.

But now I see well how I was the laughing stock of everyone for a long time, and for that I am ashamed of myself;

and of my delirium shame is the fruit, and repentance, and the clear recognition that whatever is pleasing in the world is a brief dream.

This introduction is addressed to the reader of his poems, and sets the terms for the response Petrarch aims to engage. He mentions how he hopes to find compassion in the mind of the reader who might well have had a similar experience of love. On the other hand, he makes it clear that he now realises how foolish he has made himself appear and he accepts shame and repentance as the only outcome of the experience described in his poetry. The frame established suggests an insistence on the poverty of human resources and on the essential imperfection of man, which reflects the perspective of St Augustine.

39

However, here as elsewhere in the sonnets, the focus is on the experience of love itself, and on the insistent consciousness provoked by the intensity of this experience. Although he has been a 'laughing stock' in the eyes of the world, he still hopes for a sympathetic response from readers who recognise his plight and will identify with it. Petrarch is careful not to glamorise the state of being in love. He calls it delusion. However, to acknowledge this state as an ineluctable symptom of the human condition, and to draw identification with it from the reader is in itself a token of honesty.

This introductory poem contains two perspectives; the 'before' and 'after', which again may recall Augustine's two insights, that before and that after his conversion. The sonnets which recount the full flight of passion, however, are remarkable for their capacity to recreate the moment of which they speak. The sonnet quoted below is a an example of this art:

3

Era il giorno ch'al sol si scoloraro
per la pietà des suo fattore i rai;
quando i' fui preso, e non me ne guardai,
ché i b' vostr'occhi, Donna, mi legaro.

Tempo non mi parea da far riparo
contr'a colpi d' Amor; pero m'andai
secur, senza sospetto; onde i miei guai
nel commune dolor s'incominciaro.

Trovommi Amor del tutto disarmato,
et aperta la via per gli occhi al core,
che di lagrime son fatti iuscio e varco.

40

2. Petrarch's Sonnets

Pero al mio parer, non lo fu onore
ferir me de saetta in quello stato,
a vol armata non monstrar pur l'arco.

It was on the day when the rays of the sun grew pale out of compassion for the Maker that I was captured, and I did not defend myself against it, for your beautiful eyes, Lady, bound me.

It did not seem to me a time for protecting myself against the blow of Love; therefore I went secure and without suspicion; and so my sorrows began in the midst of the common grief.

Love found me quite disarmed, and the way open through my eyes to the heart, my eyes which have become the gate and the passageway of tears.

So, as I see it, it did him no honour to wound me with his arrow while I was in that state and not even to show his bow to you, who were armed.

Here we find images which were to become seminal in their capacity to evoke the experience of being in love. Love is seen as a 'blow', which strikes when the lover is unprepared; love, traditionally Cupid with his bow, shoots an arrow through the lover's eyes, which straightaway reaches his heart. The lady's eyes are said to 'bind' him. Love, personified, is belittled for his cowardice in striking an unprepared victim. It is interesting that the terms of the encounter between Love and the lover are reminiscent of a courtly ethos: there was no 'honour' in the encounter for the assailant. On the other hand the lady, who was 'armed'; since she was invincible through her indifference, was not even shown Love's weapons. Her haughty remoteness had a greater power than Love himself.

The metaphors in this sonnet are mixed; the lover's eyes are penetrated by the arrow of love; he is 'bound' by the eyes of his beloved. Because Petrarch does not seek to establish a narrative sequence, the effect is one of vulnerability and cumulative assault It is important to realise the implications of the context Petrarch cites for the moment at which he fell in love: it is the afternoon of Good Friday, at the time when at Christ's death the sky was said to grow dark. The poet speaks of 'the common grief' when all were sorrowful at the memory of Christ's agony. Yet, the lover's own overwhelming response to meeting his love stands out against this. The encounter with Laura overshadows Christ's death. This stark contrast shows how the state of being in love has distanced the lover from the deepest truth of his faith.

In the *Canzoniere* there are many sonnets which describe the tortured restlessness of the lover's state of mind. Petrarch uses analogies with acute physical discomfort, such as freezing or burning. Antitheses are recurrent, indicating above all that the lover is unable to understand, define or restrain what is happening to him. The idiom used is in effect a challenge to the logical coherence one expects from the written word just as a surrealist painting, faultless in reproductive detail, and yet contradictory in its overall effect, throws the painter's mastery against the expectations of the viewer. The following sonnet is a good example of such striking contrasts.

134
Pace non trovo e non ó da far guerra,
e temo e spero, et ardo e son un ghiaccio,
e volo sopra'l cielo e giaccio in terra,
e nulla stringo e tutto 'l mondo abbraccio.

2. Petrarch's Sonnets

Tal m'à in pregion, che non m'apre né serra,
né per suo mi riten né scioglie il laccio,
e non m'ancide Amore e non mi sferra,
né mi vuol vivo né mi trae d'impaccio.

Veggio senza occhi e non ò lingua e grido,
e bramo di perir e cheggio aita,
et ò in odio me stesso ed amo altrui.

Pascomi di dolor, piangiendo rido,
egualmente mi spiace morte e vita:
in questo stato son, Donna, per vui.

I find no peace and have no strength to make war, and I fear and hope, I burn and am ice, and I fly above the heavens and lie upon the ground, and I grasp nothing and all the world I embrace.

One has me in prison, who neither opens nor locks the door for me, and neither keeps me as hers nor unties the bonds, and Love neither kills me nor frees me from my chains, and neither wants me alive nor rescues me from trouble.

I see without eyes I have no tongue and I cry out, I yearn to perish and I beg for help. I hate myself and love another.

I feed on pain and laugh while weeping, death and life equally displease me; in this state am I, lady, because of you.

The lover's existence and his perception of it are a source of relentless contradiction. The poem shows him to be disorientated, and totally wretched.

Petrarch's choice of recurrent antitheses set a fashion, much imitated by subsequent poets. Yet to take these antitheses out of the moral context which Petrarch's sonnets imply, is to treat them simply as amusing literary affectation. It is ironic that the predictability that this style eventually acquired, with its over-use of antithesis and examples of excessive physical discomfort, robbed such terms of their impact.

It is useful, then, to look at some sonnets where Petrarch rigorously established the perspective from which he wished the reader to see the state of mind he describes. The following does this well. Instead of suggesting that the lover is the epitome of sensitivity, he shows his mind to be *robbed* of appropriate response by his condition.

145

Ponmi ove 'l sole occide i fiori e l'erba
o dove vince lui il ghiaccio e la neve,
ponmi ov'eil carro suo temprato e leve
et ov' e chi cel rende o chi cel serba;

ponmi un umil fortuna od in superba,
al dolce aere sereno, al fosco e greve;
ponmi a la notte, al dilungo ed al breve,
a la matura etate od a l'acerba;

ponmi in cielo od in abisso,
il alto poggio, in valle ima et palustre,
libero spirto od a suoi membri affisso

pommi con fama oscura o con illustre;
sarò qual fui, vivro com'io son visso,
continuando il mio sospir trilustre.

Set me where the sun kills the flowers and the grass, or where he is vanquished by the ice and snow, set me where his chariot is temperate and light and where those people dwell who give him back to us or who keep him from us.

Set me in humble or in proud fortune, in sweet clear air, in dark and heavy; set me in the night, in the short day and the long, in mature age or in youth;

set me in heaven or on earth or in the abyss, or on a high hill, in a low marshy valley, a spirit free or tied to the body;

set me in obscurity or in illustrious renown; I shall be what I have been, I shall live as I have lived, continuing my trilustral singing.

Here, Petrarch creates the image of an extreme physical climate; a destructive heat from the sun, an icy chill; he refers to stages in social success, differences in age, in location. However, in this sonnet, he shows that the essential features of the lover's experience of life have no effect on him. Whatever the situation in which the lover finds himself, the only truth of his condition to which he admits is the compulsion to sing of his 'trilustral love' – the love that has lived through three stages since it began.

This poem suggests that, far from glorifying the mind and elevating it to rhapsodic heights, the effect of love is to render it oblivious to all experience other than the lover's passion. In Sonnet

365, he declares that his love for a mortal creature has weighed him down, preventing him from aiming for spiritual fulfilment.

> *I'vo piangendo i miei passati tempi*
> *i quai posi in amar cosa mortale,*
> *senza levarmi a volo, abbiend'io l'ale,*
> *per dar forse di me non bassi esempi.*

I go weeping for my past days which I spent in loving a mortal crea-ture, without lifting myself in flight, although I had the wings to set perhaps not a mean example of myself.

In his prose writing, Petrarch composed an imaginary dialogue between 'Francescus' and 'Augustinus', in which he gives Augustinus the following comment (Minta, 1980: 32):

Nothing so much leads a man to forget or to despise God as the love of things temporal, and most of this passion that we call love: and to which by the greatest of all desecration, we even give the name of god, without doubt only that we may throw a heavenly veil over our human follies and make a pretext of divine inspiration when we want to commit an enormous transgression.

Although Petrarch is remembered above all for celebrating the impact of passion with searing imagery, it is important to be aware of the enduring melancholy which accompanies the depiction of this intense state of mind. There is an Augustinian despair about man's capacity to control his reactions. One sonnet in particular, 132, expresses the conscious confusion which prevails in the lover's thoughts, and demonstrates the failure of his efforts to try to identify what is happening to him.

2. Petrarch's Sonnets

S'amor non e che dunquè è quel ch'io sento?
ma s'egli è amor, per Dio, che cosa et quale?
se bona, ond'el'è ffeto aspro mortale?
si ria, ond'è si dolce ogni tormento?

S'a mia voglia ardo, ond'è 'l pianto e lamento
s'a mal mio grado, il lamentar che vale?
O viva morte, o dilettosa male,
come puoi tanto in me, s'io nol consento?

En s'io 'l consento, a gran torto mi doglio.
Fra si contrari venti in frale barca
mi trovo in alto mar senza governo:

si lieve di saver, d'error si carca
ch'i' medesmo non so quel ch'io mi voglio,
e tremo a mezza state, ardendo il verno.

If it is not love, what then is it that I feel? But, if it is love, by God, what kind of thing is it? If it is good, whence comes the bitter mortal effect? If evil, why is each torment so sweet?

If of my own free will I burn, whence comes the weeping and lamentation? If against my will, what is the use of lamenting? O living death, O delicious pain, how can you exercise so much power within me if I do not consent to it?

And if I do consent to it, I am very wrong to complain. Amidst such contrary winds I find myself in a frail bark upon the open sea without a rudder:

So light of wisdom, so laden with error, that I myself do not know what I want, I shiver in midsummer while burning in winter.

47

This sonnet shows very clearly that Petrarch associates the excessive emotional vulnerability of being in love with man's lack of control over his own will. Love is shown by Petrarch as a symptom of hopeless moral confusion. The sonnet quoted above uses the familiar images of freezing and burning to express the inner moral turmoil of not knowing one's own mind.

The image created of Laura is similar in many ways to that of the remote, unyielding lady of the troubadour songs. Yet, whereas the lady in the songs of the troubadours was associated with an unattainable divine good, the love for Laura is presented by Petrarch as a distraction from this holy quest. Although, in Sonnet 159, Petrarch writes of Laura as the ideal of all beauty, suggesting that she constituted in a certain way some kind of Platonic absolute, in general the lover's submission to the power of love in Petrarch's poetry is an indication of the confined wretchedness of mortality. In Sonnet 22, he shows how, above all, man is the victim of the delusion of time. The lover hopes to be able to satisfy his amorous longing in his mortal condition, but the passing of time has no capacity to satisfy his fundamental needs. They are spiritual, and he has mistaken them as physical.

> *Quanto più n'avicino al giorno estremo*
> *che l'umana miseria suol far breve,*
> *più veggio il tempo andar veloce en leve*
> *e'l mio di lui sperar fallace en scemo.*
>
> *I dico a miei pensier; 'Non molto andremo*
> *d'amor parlando omai, ché 'l duro e greve*
> *terreno incardo, come fresca neve,*
> *si va struggendo, onde noi pace avremo.*

2. Petrarch's Sonnets

perché con lui cadrà quella speranza
che ne fe' vaneggiar si lungamente,
e'l riso e'l pianto, et la paura et l'ira:

sì vedrem chiaro poi come sovente
per le cose dubbiose altri s'avanza
e come spesso indarno si sospira.'

The closer I draw near to that final day which shortens all human misery, the more I see time running swift and free, and my hope in him empty and delusive.

I say to my thoughts:not much longer now shall we go talking of love, for the hard and grievous earthly burden, like new fallen snow is melting, and we shall have peace.

For with it will fall the hope that made us so long delirious, and the laughter and the weeping and the fear and the anger:

and we shall see clearly then how often men pursue uncertain things and how often they sigh in vain.

Petrarch's poetry took the theme of love for its substance, but the theme of life as its context. To separate his portrayal of the pain and paradox of love from his awareness of the spiritual need of the human condition is to misunderstand it.

3

Ronsard
Love of the Idiom

The High Renaissance saw a celebration of humanity, which distinguished it from the Middle Ages. Pierre de Ronsard, writing in France two hundred years later than his Italian predecessor, was known as the French Petrarch. However, the ebullience of the age in which he wrote contributed to a very different tone in his love poetry from that of Petrarch's sonnets. The identity which Ronsard presents in his poetry is bolstered by a confidence not encountered in that of Petrarch. A consideration of the social and aesthetic climate which developed in Ronsard's time helps to establish some of the causes of this change.

All public art in the Middle Ages was under the influence of the Church. Those painters who were employed by the Church, were bound to respect the established iconography in order to fulfil their commissions acceptably. However, as aristocrats and principalities grew more powerful, alternative criteria were encouraged by secular patrons; the desire for portrayal of aspects of real life in observed detail, as pursued by artists of Greece and Rome, was a stimulating aim. Artists of the Renaissance strove to present their subject matter in a new and interesting way, thus bringing more honour to their patron. The gifted artist thus found new encouragement and freedom. Poetry too was to benefit from the celebration of the resources of humanity. The new respect and encouragement for the poet which developed in the Renaissance was to make a big difference to the poet's view of the value of his writing and, indeed, of the worth of his own perceptions. The troubadours were accorded a mere entertainment value by the courts of the Middle Ages. The relatively adventurous sonnets which emerged from the court of Frederick II in Sicily in the twelfth century had a confined influence. Petrarch's personal poetry in the vernacular had less moral significance than his prose works. Poets, then, had no real status in modern Europe before the Renaissance; they were regarded with suspicion by the Church, which described them as liars. Their use of images was considered deceptive. The imagination, far from being valued as fund of creativity as it is today, was seen as the symptom of a dangerously wandering mind. However the advent of humanism, which developed amongst thinkers beyond the Church, fostered an interest in the human focus of the writings of Greece and Rome. It promoted the value of the writing of the ancients, including the ancient poets. The great early sixteenth-century Dutch humanist Erasmus, to the disapproval of his monastic superiors, taught himself Greek whilst in a Benedictine monastery and avidly digested the ancient texts. Erasmus found that reading the poetry of Homer, Virgil and Ovid formed a preparation for the development of spiritual sensitivity and responsiveness. Because Erasmus's ultimate aim was to focus on the essential truth of Christ's word in the gospels, he warned against an addiction to the aesthetic pleasures of ancient texts (he called this 'growing old on the rocks of the sirens'), and insisted that a response to the poetry of the pagans must be seen as no more than a preparation for an eventual understanding of the presence of Christ in the gospels. Erasmus's opposition to what he called the barbarism of the monasteries paved the way for a respect for the value of individual human response and expression. It also suggested that the mind which responded to the insight and verbal powers of the poetry of the ancients was privileged in its sensitivity.

Erasmus, in common with other early humanists, wrote in Latin. But later in the sixteenth century, the idea was conceived that a felicity similar to that of Greek and Roman writers might also be achieved by contemporary writers in the vernacular. This idea found favour in a climate of increasing nationalism, as individual countries and principalities sought to assert themselves as powers in their own right and not simply as offshoots of the Holy Roman Empire or as appendages to the Church. Newly nascent powers paid great attention to the revival of the legacy of Greece and Rome. In the early sixteenth century, under the influence of Francis I, education flourished in France and many centres of learning were established. One such was the Collège de Coqueret, run by Jean Dorat, an accomplished Hellenist. His pupils were much affected by Dorat's love of Greek and Latin poetry, and some of them were inspired to create a poetry in French which would contain similar qualities. They formed a group called the Pléiade. One of these poets was Joachim du Bellay. In 1549 he published a work called *La deffence et illustration de la langue francoyse*, which was designed to establish the independent value of an enlightened use of the French language. This treatise is seminal in understanding the new view of poetry and of the poet that was to generate a confident and independent creativity ; this is the confidence to be found in the work of Pierre de Ronsard, a fellow pupil of du Bellay's at the Collège de Coqueret.

The *Deffence* asserted the idea that the French language could be a valid medium for the expression of lofty concepts. Early humanists has assumed that Greek and Latin alone had this power. Aiming to impress readers who might eventually be found amongst the aristocracy, du Bellay pointed out that Greece and Rome had only achieved their fame because so many of their writers had written vividly to recall the exploits of the Greek and Roman people. France could produce its own Homer, Ovid and Cicero, he wrote, and therefore ensure a similar effect. The French language had its own individual genius, which should be harnessed and developed. Recently the Bible had been translated into French; this fact alone showed that French was rich in powers of expression. Du Bellay insisted that it is within human power to improve and expand a language.

Having emphasised the resources of the French language, and the possible glory that its development could bring to the French nation, du Bellay next set out in the *Deffence* to raise publicly the profile of the poet, both to encourage the respect of new readership and to boost the efforts of fellow poets. He insisted on the moral superiority of the poet. This was something poets should work at. He wrote that, to be worthy of their calling, poets must focus on their spiritual development. They must lead an austere life.

> ... *qui desire vivre en la memoire de la posterité doit estre comme mort en soy mesme, suer et trembler mainte fois.*

He who wishes to live and remain in the memory of posterity must be as though dead within himself; he must perspire and tremble a great deal.

Du Bellay asserted that the poet was on a higher spiritual plane than the average man, thanks to his natural gifts, which would be enhanced by his spiritual commitment. The poet had a privileged insight. The poet's gifts would be backed up by hard work and study. In this way, his observation, willpower, understanding and judgement would be developed. Du Bellay maintained that only the sound moral quality of the writer's mind would be able to develop the French language. Since the origin of language is arbitrary, so he believed, its development depended on the will power and judgement of its users.

In the course of the *Deffence*, du Bellay expressed a concept of knowledge which implicitly transferred the perception of the truth from the Church to the mind of the receptive individual. He suggested that nature and truth are linked in their own right, and that one body of truth existed. Human beings responded to this truth in different ways, and expressed their responses differently.

> ... *ainsi donques toutes les choses que la Nature a créees, tous les Ars et Sciences, en toutes les quatre parties du monde, sont chacune en soy mesme une chose, mais pource que les hommes sont de divers vouloirs ilz en parlent et escrivent diversememt.*

> ... just as all things created by nature, all the arts and sciences in all four corners of the world are all in themselves one and the same, but because men are of different minds, they speak and write of it differently.

Du Bellay's treatise is a call for respect for the writer's freedom. The French language can be used to boost the honour of France. The writers who use it have specific moral gifts, which must be respected.

Du Bellay advised the poet to enrich the French language by following the Greek authors, not by translating them, but by absorbing them, so that their own work would be enriched. These works must be thoroughly digested, and then transformed into blood and nourishment. Du Bellay praised Greek and Roman odes, designed for accompaniment by the lute; a French form of the odes would be welcome, if lavishly illustrated with erudition and reference to Greek mythology. The subject matter for poetry should be lofty, such as praise offered to the gods. Notably, du Bellay side-stepped the common conviction of the supremacy of Christianity, and suggested the suitability for poetry of a metaphysic more akin to the Greek and Roman concept of the gods and fate. Interestingly, he also recommended as suitable subjects for poetry, the preoccupation's of young men, notably love and drink.

Although du Bellay's concept of poetry was consciously erudite, based on Greek and Roman precedent, he did not wish poetry to be arid and obscure. He and his colleagues of the Pléiade strove to create a sensual poetry, appealing to the whole man, not just to the intellect. The poem must be *'esloignez du vulgaire'* – at a remove from the rabble; its sensual content should appeal only to the most cultivated sensibilities.

It is clear that the movement of the Pléiade recast the role of the poet in such a way as to magnify the poet's personal identity. This status was to prove invaluable to an ambitious young courtier, Pierre de Ronsard, who initially had no idea of becoming a poet. He was born to a noble family of the Vendômois in 1524. His father, Louis, had accompanied the sons of François I when they were taken hostage by Charles V. Louis de Ronsard was much impressed by what he glimpsed of Italian culture. He was keen that his son Pierre receive a good education. Originally he intended him to follow a military career, as he had done himself. Pierre became page to the Dauphin in 1536, and subsequently was in the service of many powerful members of the French court. However, in 1540, he contracted an illness which was to leave him deaf and consequently precluded a military career. An alternative to a military career for a young nobleman was the Church, and Ronsard received the tonsure in 1543; this committed him to a nominal celibacy, and also entitled him to various ecclesiastical benefices which would ensure an income. In 1547, Ronsard met Jean Dorat and enthusiastically pursued his classes at the Collège de Coqueret, where he met Jean du Bellay. The mould of intrinsic superiority and unparalleled value to France, in which du Bellay and the other members of the Pléiade cast the poet, made poetry seem the ideal career for the young nobleman. Ronsard's attraction to this calling shows that the qualities with which du Bellay, and indeed Ronsard himself, endowed the poet were more than compatible with the identity of the Renaissance courtier. They implied an intrinsic nobility and an implicitly indispensable value to the country. Able to raise the status of the French language to that of Greek and Latin, the poet's use of French was now a source of power. This meant that the role of a poet was now on a par with the profession of military leader, the spiritual status of a priest and the rank of an aristocrat.

The effect of this sudden apotheosis of the poet is discernible throughout Ronsard's poetry. He shows himself to be conscious of himself as a privileged artist, who, through poetry, can transform all of which he writes into something of value. He is his own arbiter, responsible to no-one's patronage but that of his own poetic calling. Ronsard was driven by a desire to explore his own genius. He was eager to adopt the forms developed by the ancients, such as the Greek ode, but he also looked for other precedents which he might turn to his own use and taste. His abiding ambition was to write a French epic, to equal Homer's *Iliad*. His tremendous creative energy led to a restlessness in production, so that the reader catches him at various stages of enthusiasm and focus. He was a writer totally preoccupied with the act of writing, which meant in a sense that his subject matter took second place. It might be suggested, therefore, that Ronsard's writing itself, and therefore his own genius, was the subject of his poetry.

Ironically, then, Ronsard's love poetry, although overtly addressed to a beloved woman, is essentially a tribute to his own genius. His brilliant use of language asserts the theme of love as valuable, because it recreates the personal response of a privileged being.

The effect of this focus can be seen through a comparison of his love sonnets with those of Petrarch. Ronsard's *Amours*, published in 1552/3, were clearly indebted to him. Rushing as they did to absorb and then build on the precedent of the ancient poets, the *Pléiade* also sought to emulate Petrarch's genius, which had brought new glory to the Italian language, just as the *Pléiade* hoped to bring to French. However, where Petrarch uses his identity as a lover to illustrate the wretched vulnerability of the human condition, Ronsard validates his experiences as a lover through his ability to transpose them into poetry. Petrarch's *Canzoniere* recount the melancholy effect of his first falling in love through until the time when, the prospect of death before him, he antici-pates peace. Ronsard's *Amours*, however, indicate a creative excitement inspired by each aspect of the experience of love, even when nominally, following the Petrarchan tradition, the experience is one of pain and confusion. Ronsard's early love sonnets have no implicit chronological structure, as do Petrarch's poems to Laura, but each stands in own right, its fierce emotive colouring a tribute to the intensity of its inspiration.

Ronsard's earliest sonnets were dedicated to Cassandre Salviati whom he met at the Château de Blois in the 1540s. However, just as Petrarch rarely refers directly to Laura, so Ronsard uses Cassandre's effect on him as the subject matter of his sonnets, rather than seeking to portray Cassandre herself. A close consideration of the first sonnet in this sequence reveals Ronsard's capacity to expand through his poetry the experience of love.

> *Qui voudra voyr comme un Dieu me surmonte,*
> *Comme il m'assault, comme il se fait vainqueur,*
> *Comme il r'enflamme, & r'englace mon coeur,*
> *Comme il reçoit un honneur de ma honte,*
> *Qui voudra voir une jeunesse pronte*
> *A suyvre en vain l'objet de son malheur,*
> *Me vienne voir: il voirra ma douleur,*
> *Et la rigueur de l'Archer qui me donte.*
> *Il cognoistra combien la raison peult*
> *Contre son arc, quand une fois il veult*
> *Que nostre coeur son esclave demeure:*
> *Et si voirra que je suis trop heureux,*
> *D'avoir au flanc l'aiguillon amoureux,*
> *Plein du venin dont il fault que je meure.*

He who wishes to see how I am overcome by a God, how he assaults me and how he conquers me, how he sets my heart alight and then freezes it again, how he draws honour from my shame; he who wishes to see youth ready to pursue in vain the cause of its misery, let him come to see me; he will see my distress, and the rigour of the Archer who overwhelms me. He will discover how little reason can do to resist his bow, once he has decided to enslave our heart. And he will also see that I am only too happy to have the arrow of love piercing my flank, filled with the poison from which I must die.

The compass of this sonnet is vast. It is written directly with the repetition of 'Qui' as a challenge to the reader, offering the persona of the poem as an example of the state to which anyone may be reduced by the onslaught of love, his conqueror. The offer is made in a spirit of defiant courage, daring the reader to witness the spectacle of the assailant's victory. The sonnet is shot through with imagery characteristic of Petrarch: flames, ice, archer, arrow. Yet, most overwhelming is the presence of the victim. The personification of love as a triumphant god serves to emphasise the passion of the victim; his experience is amplified by this combat in vigour and scope. The admission in the 'turn' of the sonnet, that the lover rejoices in this plight, represents another defiant thrust. The reader is challenged, not only to have the courage to appreciate the victimisation of the lover, but to admire his readiness to see it through. The overall impression is of the dignity of a committed soldier, wounded yet unscathed in honourable battle.

In many of the sonnets of the Cassandre cycle, Ronsard continues to borrow from Petrarch. But his restless creativity goes beyond Petrarch, and each of the sonnets possesses singular insights or ornaments. Sonnet XII, for example, plays on Cassandre's name. Her namesake was the daughter of Priam and Hecuba, the prophetess of Troy. Here, Ronsard places a curse, in her mouth, condemning his efforts to futility. The poem introduces a dramatic dimension, so that both reader and poet seem to overhear the words allegedly spoken by his prophetic mistress:

> *Avant le temps tes temples fleuriront,*
> *De peu de jours ta fin sera bornée,*
> *Avant ton soir se clorra ta journée,*
> *Trahis d'espoir tes pensers periront.*
> *Sans me flechir tes esciptz flétriront,*
> *En ton desastre ira ma destinée,*
> *Ta mort sera pour m'amour terminée,*
> *De tes soupirs tes nepveux se riront.*
> *Tu seras faict d'un vulgaire la fable*
> *Tu bastiras sur l'incertain du sable,*
> *Et vainement tu peindras dans les cieulx:*
> *Ainsi disoit la Nymphe qui m'afolle,*
> *Lorsque le ciel pour séeller sa parolle*
> *D'un dextre ésclair fut presage ames yeulx.*

Well before time, the temples will be filled with your funeral flowers; your end will be confined to a few days only, your day will close before evening falls and your thoughts will perish, all hope devastated. Without moving me, your writings will wither and your disastrous ending will ensure my fate. Your death will result from the ending of my love your nephews will mock your sighs. You will become a tale told by the rabble. You will build on the uncertainty of sand and you will paint of the heavens in vain. ' So said the Nymph who drives me mad, at the very moment when, to seal the truth of her words, heaven sent a propitious bolt of lightning to alert my eyes.

More than anything, this sonnet demonstrates the degree to which Ronsard, as poet, pays homage to his inspiration. He transforms Cassandre, his beloved, into the prophet who holds in her hands the key to his fate. Through this sleight of hand, Ronsard is able to outline the area of his own vulnerability as a poet; not only might his mistress not be moved by his writings, but these may themselves disappear altogether, leaving the poet as an object of vulgar derision. His peril is that his aspirations might be seen to have no sound foundation, and that he is dabbling in vain in matters well beyond mortal scope. Ronsard's subject here is the exhilarating risk that he is taking as a writer. However, since the reader is at one with him in contemplating the threat of his art's consignment to oblivion, the effect is to enrol his reader as ally. The reader's response to the poet's account of his vulnerability, ironically, may therefore serve to ensure the permanence of the poet's gift. Ronsard's identity once more emerges enhanced, as he succeeds in promoting the durability of his poetry through the poetry itself.

Forgoing what might eventually become a crippling repetition of Petrarch's imagery, Ronsard turns to myth to enrich his sonnets. Although nominally the theme of the Cassandre cycle, as in Petrarch's sonnets to Laura, is the remoteness of his beloved, and her refusal to respond to the poet's courtship, the luxuriant richness of Ronsard's text serves to emphasise the pleasure brought him by her imaginary presence. Sonnet XIV serves to illustrate the enriching power of myth, and also the sensual pleasure derived by the poet's ability to summon the hypothetical delights of his mistress's body.

> *Je vouldroy bien, richement jaunissant*
> *En pluye d'or goute à goute descendre*
> *Dans le beau sein de ma belle Cassandre,*
> *Lors qu'en ses yeulx le somme va glissant.*
> *Je vouldroy bien en toreau blandissant*

3. Ronsard

Me transformer pour finement la prendre,
Quand elle va par l'herbe la plus tendre
Seule à l'escart mille fleurs ravissant.
Je vouldroy bien afin d'aiser ma peine
Estre un Narcisse, & elle une fontaine,
Pour m'y plonger une nuict à sejour:
Et vouldray bien que ceste nuict encore
Durast tousjours sans que jamais l'Aurore
D'un front nouveau nous r'allumast le jour.

I should love in a rich yellow shower of golden rain to fall drop by drop into the beautiful breast of my lovely Cassandre, just when drowsiness slips into her eyes. I should love to transform myself into a gleaming bull, in order to take her when she wanders through the tenderest grass, alone and private, the wonder of a thousand flowers. I should love, in order to ease my suffering, to be Narcissus and she a fountain so that I might plunge into her one night to stay. I should love this night to last for ever, without Dawn lighting day with a new face.

This sonnet owes its impact to the force of its collected mythological references. The first lines recall Jupiter's seduction of Danae, when he appeared to her, disguised as a shower of rain. The sonnet moves on to evoke Jupiter's seduction of Europa in the form of a bull. Finally, Ronsard identifies with Narcissus, who fell in love with his own reflection as he contemplated it in a stream. Evocation of these myths may be said to give the poem a cultural status; it shows off the poet's classical education, at a time when to do so was widely appreciated. But the myths also enable the poet to convey a vivid account of physical contact with his beloved. He evokes the drops of rain falling into Cassandre's breast, and identifies himself with this intimacy. The image of the bull, taking Cassandre as she walks alone in the fields, allows Ronsard the licence of envisaging the most outrageous rape, oddly legitimised by the reference to Jupiter. Finally, the image of Narcissus plunging into his own reflection evokes more than any previous figure in this poem the intense self-indulgence of his love. Cassandre emerges as the mirror of his passion, which he seeks ever to intensify. The effect of writing poetry, of course, is this very intensification.

Ronsard's sonnets to Casssandre expand his identity as lover and poet, elevating his cultural status through reference to history and to myth. But their impact derives in particular from his ability to recreate the delights of physical love. Although these early sonnets are amongst the most erudite, their impact derives from the passions they evoke. The reader's response, once he has picked up the clues, is probably not primarily cerebral. Yet the exhilarating humanity of the experience of these sonnets is as much a tribute to the power of poetry itself as to their evocation of passionate desire.

Ronsard's joy in the expanding of his poetic prowess led to a radical change of style in his love poetry. His *Continuation des Amours*, published in 1555, is overtly addressed to a different woman: Marie, a country girl. However, the change of addressee in these sonnets means less here than do other changes that he now introduces. Ronsard apparently now sought to describe a different kind of relationship. Although he had expanded his imagery beyond the Petrarchan in the Cassandre cycle, the terms of the relationship which implicitly governed them had been the same as those between Petrarch and Laura: he loved, she refused. The tensions brought about by this irreconcilable stance had created the structure of most of the Cassandre sonnets, but as Ronsard's confidence grew, he realised that, although Petrarch might have sufficed as his first model, he had himself moved on, not least in the emphasis on the delights of imminent physicality, rather than the distress of a bereft state of mind. His increased confidence thus led him to take up a relatively unadorned style. He now writes of a relationship in which love is reciprocated. The complex, erudite images which lend force to the Cassandre sonnets are set aside to make way for images drawn from nature and an immediate contact with the beloved. The tension of the Petrarchan concept of an interior ironic pleasure drawn from pain vanishes, and instead the reader is drawn into a pleasurable extroverted intimacy which the lovers share.

In fact, Ronsard took up his new '*style bas*', the 'low style', before he abandoned his addresses to Cassandre, and we find, rather surprisingly, poems to Cassandre in what appears to be a highly incongruous style, especially if they are seen in comparison with the preceding sonnets of the collection. The following ode published in 1553, provides a good example of this disparity:

> *Mignonne, allons voir si la rose*
> *Qui ce matin avoit declose*
> *Sa robe de pourpre au soleil,*
> *A point perdu, cette vesprée*
> *Les plis de sa robe pourprée,*
> *Et son teint au vostre pareil.*
> *Las, voiés comme en peu d'espace,*
> *Mignonne, elle a dessus la place*
> *Las, las ses beautés laissé cheoir!*
> *O vraiment maratre Nature,*

Puis qu'une telle fleur ne dure
Que du matin jusques au soir.
  Donc, si vous me croiés, mignonne,
Tandis que vôtre age fleuronne
En sa plus verte nouveauté,
Cueillés, cueillés vôtre jeunesse
Comme a cette fleur, la vieillesse
Fera ternir vôtre beauté.

My sweet, let us go and see if the rose, which this morning revealed her purple robe to the sun, has not this evening lost the folds of her purpled dress and her colour fine as yours. Alas, behold how in such a short time she has seen her beauties fall! O, what a wicked step-mother is Nature, who doesn't allow a flower to last from the morning until evening! Therefore, if you believe me, my sweet, while you are in the flower of your youth and in its greenest freshness, pluck, pluck your youth since, as it has done to this flower, age will wither your beauty.

This little ode marks a great turning point, which will be followed through in the *Continuation des Amours*, now addressed to Marie. In the above ode to Cassandre there are many features present which will characterise these new sonnets. Cassandre is for instance addressed directly. The invitation to inspect the rose forms part of an implicit immediate relationship; the tone of the verse is conversational, and the lament inspired by the fading of the rose is offered as part of a shared experience. Admittedly, the theme is the commonplace *carpe diem*, yet the elegant tenderness with which it is expressed gives it a fresh impact. The repetition of 'mignonne' also provides a gentle musicality.

All these features can be found in the subsequent *Continuation des Amours* cycle where the focus is exclusively on the immediacy of the contact between the lovers. No longer do these sonnets offer an introspective account of the condition of the rejected lover, or the fruits of his seductive imagination. In the Marie cycle, the reader is enjoined to be present at tender exchanges, as Marie's apparent encouragement of her lover's advances lead to a harmonious response from both.

XXXVIII

Mignonne, levés-vous, vous estes paresseuse,
Ja la gaye alouette au ciel a fredonné,
Et ja le rossignol frisquement jargonné,
Dessus l'espine assis, sa complainte amoureuse.
Debout donq, allons voir l'herbelette perleuse,
Et vostre beau rosier de boutons couronné,
Et vos oeillets aimés, ausquels avés donné
Hyer au soir de l'eau d'une main si songneuse.
   Hyer en vous couchant, vous me fistes promesse
D'estre plus(-)tost que moi ce matin eveillée,
Mais le sommeil vous tient encor toute sillée:
   Ian, je vous punirai du peché de paresse
Je vois baiser cent fois vostre oeil, vostre tetin,
Afin de vous aprendre a vous lever matin.

My sweet, get up, you are lazy. The gay skylark has warbled in the sky and the nightingale has sung sitting above the rose tree its long lament. Up then, let us go and see the grass wet with pearls of dew, and your lovely rose tree crowned with buds, and your beloved carnations, which you watered yesterday evening with such an attentive hand. Yesterday when you went to bed you promised me that you would wake this morning earlier than I. But sleep still closes your eyelids together. Well, I'll punish you for your sin of laziness, I shall kiss your eyes and your breasts a hundred times to teach you to get up in the morning.

As the reader cannot fail to notice, this sonnet is no more than elegant *badinage* in which the lover teases his mistress. There is no moral axiom, as in the *carpe diem* ode to Cassandre; the whole implicit dialogue is lighthearted, and decorated with the imagery of birds and flowers. It is easy to see why Ronsard was able to write to du Bellay that nothing came more naturally to him than love; at this point he rejoiced in the spontaneity of his sexuality and of his poetry. He was so convinced of the intrinsic superiority of his identity, that his own response to things clearly dictated their worth. The death of Marie inspired him with a poetic reflection on death which was interchangeable with his response to the death of Henri III. He is now the subject of the impulse of his feelings, rather than the subject of a monarch.

Twenty years later, Ronsard wrote another sonnet sequence; this time dedicated to Hélène de Surgères. There is a substantial difference in the tone and approach of these sonnets from those of the previous cycles, which suggests that a further dimension of the subject of love had occurred to him. The poet is no longer obsessed with the aesthetic experience of love, rivalled only by writing of it, as in the Cassandre sequence. Neither does the relatively calm and bucolic frame of mind, discernible in the Marie cycle, form part of this love poetry. Instead, we find in his sonnets to Hélène a reflection of the irregularities of an unstable relationship. He is openly critical of Hélène in his verse, accusing her of disdain; not so much in the lofty tradition of courtly love, but more in terms of her petty vanity. Occasionally he is hostile, likening her to Pandora, whose box let out elements that would be the scourge of mankind. In Sonnet LXIII, he makes it clear that he no longer feels swept on to his passion by an irresistible force. The terms in which he describes his attachment to Hélène relate more to his personal taste and judgement:

LXIII

Vous seule me plaisez: j'ay par election,
Et non a la volée aimé vostre jeunesse:
Aussi je prins en gré toute ma passion.
Je suis de ma fortune autheur, je le confesse.
La vertu m'a conduit en telle affection:
Si la vertu me trompe, adieu belle Maitresse.

You alone please me, I have loved your youth through choice and not at random: so I welcomed all my passion, I am author of my fate, I admit it. Virtue led me to feel so deeply. If Virtue has deceived me, farewell lovely mistress.

The terms of the relationship which forms the axis of these sonnets are very different from those of the Cassandre and Marie cycles. In the sonnets to Hélène, the poet presents himself as in control. He delights in Hélène's youth, he is impatient with her petulance. But, above all, he is aware of himself as on a completely different plane from his mistress. Hélène is of the world, whereas the passion he recounts for Cassandre was the motive force in lifting the poet beyond the world, so that he was free to enjoy a series of rhapsodic aesthetic experiences. The relationship described with Marie depicted the lovers sharing, on equal intimate terms, their delight in nature and in their love. However, the Hélène cycle implies that the poet's paramount existence is apart from the woman he loves, morally and spiritually. One of Ronsard's best-known sonnets suggests this difference profoundly:

LXXV

Quand vous serez bien vieille, au soir á la chandelle,
Assise aupres du feu, devidant & filant,
Direz, chantant mes vers, en vous esmerveillant,
Ronsard me celebroit du temps que j'estois belle.

Lors vous n'aurez servante oyant telle nouvelle,
Desja sous le labeur àdemy sommeillant,
Qui, au bruit de Ronsard ne s'aille resveillant
Benissant vostre nom de louange immortelle.

Je seray sous la terre, & fantaume sans os
Par les ombres Myrtheux je prendray mon repos.
Vous serez au fouyer une vieille accroupie,
Regrettant mon amour et vostre fier desdain.
Vivez, si m'en croyez, n'attendez à demain:
Cueillez dés aujourd'huy les roses de la vie.

When you are very old, lit by candlelight in the evening, sitting by the fire, separating the strands of wool and weaving, you will say to yourself as you recite my verses and marvel at them: Ronsard sang my praises when I was beautiful.

Then no servant of yours hearing this cry, already half asleep under her task, will fail to be roused immediately by the name of Ronsard, blessing your name with eternal praise.

I shall be beneath the ground, and, a ghost without bones, I shall enjoy repose in the myrtle shades. You will be a withered old crone by the hearth, missing my love and regretting your fierce pride.

70

3. Ronsard

Live now, believe me, don't wait until tomorrow. Pluck the roses of life today.

Here once more is the commonplace *carpe diem* theme. Yet the impetus of the poem is less ostensibly the delights of the present moment, than the poet's power to ensure the survival of his mistress's beauty through his poetry, which, unlike Helene herself, is exempt from the ravages of time. The sonnet creates a picture of her as an aged crone bent by the fireside. He, the poet, is free, and endures in a privileged spiritual existence. The dichotomy between the two of them could not be clearer; despite Hélène's youth, her existence is bound by time and decay. He, the poet, on the other hand, is immune to such threats. His demand is less that his mistress pluck the rose of the present moment, than that his reader acquiesce before his indisputable greatness.

The success of Ronsard's love poetry lies in its variety. The writer responds to the terms of his craft. There is no indication that he, like Petrarch, sought to wrestle with the terms of his existence. Ronsard was a priest; the account of his loves could not properly be read as autobiographical. Since this account was presented exclusively as poetic material, there is no apparent tension between the love recounted in his sonnets and Ronsard's role as a priest. Although he wrote lengthy poems defending the Catholics in the civil wars, Ronsard's Christian faith seems to have had no presence in his poetic life. In keeping with du Bellay's recommendation, he found his identity as a poet confirmed metaphysically by the notion of 'divine fury', which had spread to the Pléiade from the neo-Platonic writings of Marsilio Ficino. Ficino wrote an important commentary on Plato's *Symposium*, in which he ascribed to natural, instinctive love a philosophical status hitherto unknown in modern European culture. Ficino ascribed to the soul an aspiration to reunify itself with the divinity; he saw it as subject to a natural movement leading to self-transcendence. Love and poetry were forces which stimulated this movement. Ficino said nothing in this commentary about the roles of nature and grace, as a Christian perspective would demand. His philosophical stance therefore offered the imaginative writer huge scope for a confidence in the metaphysical validity of his gifts as a writer, and of his experience of passion. Ronsard settled happily into this appreciation of his art. Perhaps, however, Ronsard was inspired less by the need for self-transcendence, as by his yearning for self-fulfilment on an aesthetic and a social level.

4

The Idiom of Folly
Louise Labé

Pierre de Ronsard drew from the cultural ferment of the High Renaissance an elegant and plausible way of presenting his identity as a poet. His knowledge of classical precedents and the growing respectability of the vernacular entitled him to an aristocratic freedom amidst the cultural élite of France. The tensions within his work were those that he chose for aesthetic reasons. However, in Lyons, a cultural corridor between France and Italy, there were equally interesting developments. A notable poet of this period was Louise Labé, a rope maker's daughter. She was by no means born into the aristocracy as was Ronsard, but she was clearly in touch with the intellectual life of Lyons, which at this time was a major centre of printing. Little is known about her education, but her published work indicates that she was widely read, in contemporary works as well as classical texts. In the 1550s, Louise wrote love sonnets. These were and are remarkable in that they present a female persona as the lover. Louise knew Petrarch's sonnets well and borrowed from them the imagery of physical distress to invoke the mental state of the lover. However, the theme of female vulnerability provided a fascinating addition to the love interest of the sonnet; the narrow line between the newly established dignity of the perceptive poet and the shame of

73

the exposed woman was a galvanising point of tension. Louise's sonnets were innnovative and powerful. Clearly, it would be possible to examine them in the same way as Ronsard's *Amours*, deducing from within each sonnet the poetic skills of the poet. However, Louise also left us with a discussion of the effects of passion on the human condition. This reveals much about how the lover's state of mind was understood in the climate of Renaissance humanism. Her *Débat de Folie et d'Amour* (Debate between Folly and Love), written in 1552, presents the concept of love against a broad philosophical and moral background. This background is wider than the range of concepts selected to promote the cause of poetry by Ronsard and du Bellay. It is immensely rewarding to follow the arguments in Louise's satirical debate, and only then to re-read some of her sonnets in the light of its conclusions.

Louise was apparently familiar with Homer, Plato, Lucian and Sappho, and also with works that had recently appeared in the publishing houses of Lyons, such as the translation of Erasmus's *Encomium Moriae* (*In Praise of Folly*), in which Erasmus mocked the emptiness of human pretensions. She was also conscious of the early fiction of Rabelais, in which an authentic popular idiom of writing was taking hold. All these texts contain intrinsic challenges to the esoteric refinements of those writers interested only in reproducing the classical paradigm. The *Débat* bears traces of the influence of many satiric writers, ancient and modern. However, its interest does not lie merely in its allusions. It is written is a highly imaginative and lively style which, in itself, is a disclaimer to academic pretension. The intention of the style is clearly to suggest immediacy. The squabble between Cupid and Folly, with which the *Débat* begins, is reminiscent of the quarrel between the cake bakers and the grape harvesters in Rabelais's *Gargantua*, a trivial episode which led to great wars. As in that quarrel, the level of discussion does not rise above insult and arrogance. The debate in Louise's text is then transferred to Jupiter's court, where the merits of the opposing parties, Love and Folly, are, by his command, presented by disinterested representatives: Apollo and Mercury. Debates between opposing parties were commonly presented for entertainment in the Middle Ages (one such dispute was '*lequel vaut mieux à aimer du clerc ou du chevalier?*', 'which is it better to love, the cleric or the knight?'). However, although at first sight Louise's *Débat* might appear similarly fatuous, the argument proceeds along lines more suggestive of the recent *In Praise of Folly* by the Dutch humanist Erasmus. Indeed, irony is a specific feature of Louise's *Débat*. From it emerges an enlightening and objective perspective on the human susceptibility to amorous passion.

The arguments presented by Apollo to assert the supremacy of love show it as essentially altruistic. Apollo assures his audience that love is the soul of the universe, as Plato describes it in the *Symposium*. He presents it as the force that binds communities. Those who set an example of loving kindness are themselves revered by others. Men are:

> ... *ensemble liez es assemblez par une benivolence, qui les fait vouloir bien l'un a l'autre: et ceus qui en ce sont les plus excellens, sont les plus reverez entre eus.* (DFA 68)

> ... bound together in communities by a benevolent power which has made them wish one another well; and those who are the most excellent among them are the most revered.

Apollo claims that love has a morally elevating power which helps men to lead better lives. It links and unifies people. It raises their incentive to behave well, in order that they themselves might be loved. Apollo defines the desire to be loved as a universal trait, except in the case of the misanthropist, whom he proceeds to exemplify in a vivid portrayal of a grumpy, miserable recluse. Love is shown as a force that prompts civilised behaviour. It is associated with the beauty of spring, which nurtures it. Apollo claims that love invented music:

> *et est le chant et harmonie l'effect et le signe de l'Amour parfaict.*
> (DFA 75)

and song and harmony are the effect and sign of perfect Love.

Love is shown as the source of all positive experiences in human existence. On a personal level, it brings profit and pleasure; on a social level, glory and honour.

The account of love as a fundamental unifying force had been related to Christianity by Ficino in his commentary on Plato's *Symposium*, written in 1474. Ficino's neo-Platonism was designed primarily to promote the Christian concept of love. Louise's awareness of the relevance of St. Paul's First Letter to the Corinthians in which love is defined (1 Corinthians, 13, 4: '*la charite ne cherche pas son propre avantage*', 'charity vaunteth not itself') has been made clear before Apollo embarks on his defence of Cupid. Amour himself speaks of:

> *la vraye et entiere Amour qui ne cherche son proufit, mais celui de la persone, qu'il ayme.* (DFA 63)

true and whole Love which does not seek its own advantage, but that of the beloved person.

4. The Idiom of Folly

This Christian definition of love announces a fragmentation which is to occur in the course of Apollo's speech. There a dual focus emerges in his presentation of love. On the one hand, it is described as altruistic and deferential to the needs of others. On the other, it is shown to be self-seeking. Never is this rift more obvious than when Apollo quotes again from the *Symposium*:

> *entre les hommes Amour cause une connoissance de soy mesme.* (ibid.)

> amongst men, Love brings about self-knowledge.

Apollo proceeds to qualify this self-knowledge as an awareness of the image that one creates in the eyes of others:

> *celui qui desire plaire, incessamment pense a son fait.* (ibid.)

> He who desires to please thinks incessantly of the effect he has.

Apollo then goes on to give details of the efforts to which people go to improve their appearance and to hit the heights of fashion to ensnare the beloved. There is already a note of irony in his description of the extremes to which women will go in order to conserve the beauty of their face:

> *Laquelle, si elle est belle, elles contregardent tant bien contre les pluies, vents, chaleurs, tems et vieillesse.* (DFA 74-75)

> who, to ensure its beauty, guard themselves well against rains, wind, heat, time and age.

77

However, in spite of Apollo's admission of the degree of self-regard that love inspires, his final contention is that any interference on the part of folly in the affairs of love must be quashed. Such interference would inevitably lead to disaster, since it would precipitate a total lack of control. Relationships would be incongruous, since they would no longer be restrained by shame. This could lead to quarrels, even to incest! Apollo prays to Jupiter that love's presence in the lives of men should be peaceful. Lovers should be respected and regarded as trustworthy. Love should be the predominant force in human affairs, and, in order to remain so, should be clear-sighted. Blind Cupid's eyes should be returned to him.

Mercury's rejoinder to Apollo's defence of love is not the polarised account of folly's virtues which might have been expected in the traditional medieval debate. Instead, he declares that there is no quarrel at all. Basically, love and folly are friends:

> *Folie n'est rien inferieure à Amour. Amour ne seroit rien sans elle.*
> (DFA 85)

> Folly is in no way inferior to Love. Love would be nothing without her.

Mercury presents a profile of flawed humanity, showing that all human perception is founded in folly. This perspective is greatly indebted to Erasmus's *In Praise of Folly*, which shows men to be fundamentally deluded about their moral identity. Mercury demonstrates how concepts of power arise merely from ambition:

> *Folie ha premierement mis en teste à quelcun de se faire creindre. Folie ha fait les autres obéïr. Folie ha inventé toute l'excellence, magnificence, et grandeur, qui depuis à cette cause s'est ensuivie.* (DFA 86)

4. *The Idiom of Folly*

Folly first put the idea into someone's head to frighten others. Folly
compelled others to obey. Folly invented all the excellence, magnif-
icence and greatness, which since then has come into being.

Mercury shows human beings as intrinsically pretentious, reluctant
to admit their limitations, lacking humility and obsessed by the
phantom of worldly success. Mercury's dismissal of human
achievement is sweeping. Diogenes, he says, was clearly foolish, as
were all philosophers. Their brains were intrinsically deficient:

*Combien y ha il d'autres sciences au monde, lesquelles ne sont que
pure resverie?* (DFA 87)

How much more worldly knowledge is there, which could be called
nothing but dreams alone?

If folly were chased from the world, he continues, there would be
no lawyers, doctors or perfume makers. On the other hand, folly
is to be praised for the dynamism she provides which causes
human beings to enjoy life. Basically, folly makes things fun. She
lies behind myriad projects on which people embark, like the
construction of crazy and magnificent buildings, like pyramids and
amphitheatres. She persuades men to travel, when it is clearly
more sensible not to:

*Et de cette magnifique folie en demeure un long tems grand plaisir
entre les hommes, qui se destournent de leur chemin, font voyages
expres, pour avoir le contentement de ces vieilles folies.* (DFA 90-91)

And thanks to this magnificent folly, great pleasure for a long time
fills the hearts of men, who turn aside from their paths, who deliberately set out on journeys, in order to enjoy these good old sports.

Mercury adds that nothing positive would ever come about, if Jupiter were not able to create good from what men had muddled completely.

Erasmus's salutary presentation of human delusions of adequacy, compensated by grace alone, finds its echo here. But the most developed section of Mercury's argument is devoted to what he describes as the inevitable fusion of folly with love. He presents amorous passion as a folly which is a definitive feature of the human condition. Passion can be concealed but not defeated:

> *Que tant de grans personnages, qui ont esté et sont de present, ne s'estiment estre injuriez, si pour avoir aymé je les nomme fols. Qu'ils se prennent à leurs Filozofes, qui ont estimé Folie estre privacion de sagesse, et sagesse estre sans passions: desquelle Amour ne sera non plus tot destitué, que la Mer d'ondes et vagues:* (DFA 93)

> May those who have been and are yet great people not feel offended if, because they have loved, I call them mad. May they blame their philosophers, who have esteemed Folly to be a deprivation of wisdom, and wisdom to be without passions; of which love will no more be deprived than the sea of waves.

Folly is endemic to the passion of love. Attempts to suppress it are as vain as any other attempt to suppress one's humanity. Mercury contests the assertion that to be wise is to be without passion. Such self-deception can only lead to wretchedness. Mercury concedes that the effects of love on any human being are incapacitating:

> *Il faut confesser qu'incontinent que cette passion vient saisir l'homme, elle l'altere et immue.* (DFA 99)

4. *The Idiom of Folly*

It must be admitted that as soon as this passion gets a hold on man,
it changes him and fixes him.

Mercury points out that falling in love cannot be attributed to
circumstance; it must result from some intrinsic folly. He reminds his
audience of Gnidien, who fell in love with a statue. He invokes
Narcissus, who fell in love with his own reflection. There is no explanation for the *'force d'un oeil'* (the moment when the lover's glance
pierces the lover's soul). Taking up the Petrarchan image of the arrow,
Mercury claims that it will only lodge in hearts prepared for it by
folly – that is to say, by the natural propensity of human beings.
Mercury relates in detail the effects of the folly of amorous passion.
He describes the lover's inarticulacy; he is so overwhelmed that he
cannot express his feelings. Nevertheless, he seeks out an occasion to:

> ... *expliquer ses passions par soupirs et paroles tremblantes: redire
> cent fois une mesme chose: protester, jurer, promettre à celle qui
> possible ne s'en soucie, et est tournee ailleurs et promise.* (DFA 94)

> ... tell of his passions with sighs and faltering words, by repeating
> the same thing a hundred times over, protesting, swearing, vowing
> to a woman who quite possibly is totally indifferent, and is turned
> towards another to whom she is already promised.

Mercury speaks of the *'sottes et plaisantes Amours vilageoises'*
where the victims get drunk and link their name with that of their
lover, dipping a finger in wine and writing on the table. He tells of
lovers waiting all day to see the beloved and, rewarded by a little
smile, returning home as happy as Ulysses when he again saw the
smoke from the hearths of his village. If a situation gives rise to jealousy, Mercury continues, the lover's affliction is total. At first he is

81

overwhelmed by his own inadequacies, comparing himself unfavourably with his rival. He then comes to despise his rival, thinking it impossible that his own intense passion could be equalled. Apart from the distress of jealousy, the lover is highly vulnerable to the aberrations of his beloved's behaviour and is constantly ill at ease. He takes huge risks and often finds himself in compromising situations:

Les plus grandes et hazardeuses folies suivent tousjours l'acroisse-
ment d'Amour.

The greatest and most hazardous follies always follow the onset of love.

After such tension, frustration and distress, the lover might well give up. Having sighed and cried for a very long time, he might leave the country, or die, or become a monk.

To this point, the exposition of folly's intercession in matters of love has covered only the behaviour of men. But next, Mercury focuses on women, with all the more impact after his lengthy description of the inanity of their admirers. To those expecting a relatively uncritical description of the objects of male admiration, a swift rebuff is given:

Et penseriez vous, que les amours de femmes soient de beaucoup
plus sages? (DFA 96)

And would you imagine that the loves of women are far wiser?

Mercury goes on to demolish the image created in the songs of the troubadours and the sonnets of Petrarch of woman as an unresponsive, remote paragon of virtue. Those women who appear coldest, says Mercury, '*se laissent brusler dedens le corps avant que de rien avouer*' (allow themselves to burn within their bodies, before they will admit anything). They resist what they really long for, which is to be taken by force. He describes the paradox of women who insist on creating misery both for their lovers and for themselves by this refusal. When ultimately they admit their vulnerability, Mercury claims, they may still resist consummation of love until they are withered and debilitated. They allow only one conqueror and that is time itself.

On the other hand, if women acknowledge their passion and consent to an affair, matters turn out as bad as or worse than their original inhibitions caused them to fear. They are led to abandon all their household duties, to set aside their sewing and their weaving, and care only to be at feasts and at banquets, dressed in their most beautiful clothes so as to meet the object of their passion. Some women abandon father, mother, husband and children so as to be with their lover. And, worst of all, it often turns out that the more a woman loves, the more likely she is not to be loved in return. In this case, she loses all pleasure in life. Such women are ready, like Orpheus, to descend to hell to try to recover their lost love. Any token they have retained from their lover's presence, they flood with tears, or rest their cheek on it throughout the night. Their emotional state is utterly out of control. Here, avers Mercury, is incontrovertible evidence of madness. He lists its recognisable effects:

Avoir le coeur separé de soymesme, estre meintenant en paix, ores en guerre, orres en treves: courir et cacher sa douleur; changer visage mile fois le jour: sentir le sang qui lui rougit la face, y montan; puis

soudein s'enfuit, la laissant palle, ainsi que honte, esperance, ou peur,
nous gouvernent: chercher ce qui nous tourmente, feignant le fuir, et
neanmoins avoir creinte de le trouver: n'avoir qu'un petit ris entre mil
soupirs: se tromper soy mesme: bruler de loin, geler de pres: un parler
interrompu: un silence venant tout à coup: ne sont ce tous signes
d'un homme aliené de son bon entendement? (DFA 98)

To have the heart separated from oneself, to be one moment at
peace, the next at war, the next in truce; to rush away to hide one's
grief; to change expression a thousand times a day; to feel the blood
mount which brings a blush to her cheeks, then to feel it drain away,
to the degree in which shame, hope or fear gain ascendance; to go
in pursuit of what torments us, pretending to fly from it, and nevertheless be fearful of finding it; to have only a little laugh amongst a
thousand sighs; to deceive oneself; to burn at a distance, freeze
when close; to interrupt one speech, suddenly to be smitten by
silence; are not all these signs of a man bereft of sound understanding?

Mercury concludes with a final derogatory comment which,
according to him:

dure par ignorance, nonchailance, esperance, et cecité, qui sont toutes
damoiselles de Folie, lui faisans ordinaire compagnie. (DFA 102)

lasts through ignorance, indifference, hope and blindness, which
are all handservants of Folly, normally keeping her company.

He adds that it is better that love should remain blind, to spare
lovers insights into the hopelessness of its consequences.

This portrait of the condition of the lover is fascinating on many
levels. Perhaps its chief interest lies in its departure from medieval

convention. The lover is not seen here as the exponent of a particular humour who, because of the extremes of a melancholic
temperament, is unable to participate in the high-minded purposes
of life. Instead he – or she – is shown as an exponent of the fallibility of the human condition. The passion of love, as Mercury
describes it, is no greater a delusion than other aspects of human
folly, such as ambition and power. These were exposed by
Erasmus, and are dwelt on by Mercury with equal derision. The
delusion of love, like paradoxical delusions of grandeur, is rooted
in the inadequacy of human self-perception. Although there is no
evidence that Louise was directly involved in the evangelical
humanism promoted by Erasmus, there is every reason to see his
influence on the perspective adopted in the *Débat*.

Apollo's speech initially sets out to extol the altruism of love,
but subsequently describes it as contributing merely to individual
pride and flaunting. This division indicates a vast chasm between
the selfless ideal of love as expressed by Plato in the *Symposium*
which was later adopted by Ficino in his Christian commentary,
and the predatory love, which, according to Mercury's account,
obsesses most human beings. This obsession indicates their lack of
self-knowledge, their preoccupation with their own desires, their
lack of humility, and, above all, their tendency to ruin their own
lives through their enslavement to passion. The human being
presented here in Louise's *Débat* is very close to Erasmus's concept
of a fragmented humanity, unable either to perceive or to act upon
the truth of its own condition without Grace. Mercury's remark
that Jupiter alone is capable of putting right what man has marred
strongly reflects Erasmus's emphasis on the need of reference to
Christ to make sense of anything. Human resources alone are
insufficient and often deceptive.

Another interesting aspect of Mercury's description of the effects of love is the psychological perception which runs throughout his speech. He does not draw on the lexicon established by courtly love, or on that of Petrarch. Instead, his illustration emerges from observation, of which Louise had great store, moving as she did in the social circles of Lyons. For readers of Louise's sonnets, in which the persona of the lover is ostensibly the writer, the comments on the behaviour of women in love are particularly informative. Mercury's speech quoted above appears to include Louise herself in the women derided. The third person plural is abandoned for the first person plural as Mercury speaks of the colour of the lover's face turning from scarlet to pale:

> *... ainsi que honte, esperance ou peur nous gouvernenent.* (DFA 98)

> ... to the degree that shame, hope or fear gain ascendance.

He says of women in love that they try to:

> *... cercher ce qui nous tourmente, feignant le fuir, et neanmoins avoir creinte de le trouver.* (ibid.)

> ... go in pursuit of what torments us, pretending to fly from it, and nevertheless, being fearful of finding it.

References to the woman as a poet clearly point to Louise's self-awareness in this text. In *In Praise of Folly*, Erasmus mocked scholars for ruining their eyesight when they read late into the night in the way that he did himself. So Louise often mocks the woman poet.

Plusieurs femmes, pour plaire aleurs Poëtes amis, ont changé leurs paniers et coutures, en plumes et livres. (DFA 100)

Many women, in order to please their male poet friends, have swapped their basket weaving and embroidery for pens and books.

A similar telling comment comes earlier in the text, when Mercury describes the erratic behaviour of women obsessed by a lover. They close the door on reason:

Elles prennent la plume et le lut en main: escrivent et chantent leurs passions. (DFA 97)

They take pen and lute in their hand and write and sing of their passion.

It is interesting that writing poetry is presented here as evidence of dementia rather than as a noble pursuit.

The sonnets published three years after she wrote the *Débat* are a far cry from the inarticulate lover described by Mercury. They demonstrate a skill and control as impressive as that of any of her contemporaries. Yet it seems clear from the *Débat* that the state of mind they illustrate was not in itself admirable in her eyes. For every ounce of poetic craft displayed in her poetry, which commanded admiration, the content of her love sonnets can be seen from the perspective of the *Débat* as sheer folly.

However, is the contrast between the idiom of satire and that of the sonnet so acute? The sonnet was perhaps the ideal medium for an expression of an ironic perspective. Its success lies in its ability to draw the reader into identification with its first premise, and subsequently to present the adjustment contained in the concluding sestet, managing both with equal plausibility. As a consequence, the reader can be drawn into an acknowledgement of the ironic paradox of reality and the power of irony. More to the point is that Louise's sonnets are not necessarily, like those of Ronsard to be read as a celebration of the poet's response to the theme of love. Read together with the *Débat de Folie et d'Amour*, they emerge as a vivid description in imagery and self-defeating thought patterns of a particular experience, which is ultimately revealed to be an example of the paradoxical nature of the human condition.

Read alongside Mercury's ironic presentation of women in love in the *Débat*, Louise's sonnets can be seen as reflections of the states of mind that Mercury invokes. His speech is objective, almost clinical in its approach. One might see it, in modern terms, as a psychologist's report. The sonnets portray the states of mind described in his speech, but from the point of view of the person experiencing them, in other words, of the patient. If they are read in this way, the implicit irony of the poet's self-awareness emerges as a challenge posed by the actual experience.

One particular sonnet illustrates this point well, although the choice is arbitrary, since all Louise's sonnets portray a wrestling with the effects of passion, in which the subject is the instigator as well as the victim:

IV

Depuis qu'Amour cruel empoisonna
Premierement de son feu ma poitrine,
Tousjours brulay de sa fureur divine,
Qui un seul jour mon coeur n'abandonna.

4. The Idiom of Folly

Quelque travail, dont assez me donna,
Quelque menasse et procheine ruïne:
Quelque penser de mort qui tout termine
De rien mon coeur ardent ne s'estonna.

Tant plus qu'Amour nous vient fort assaillir
Plus il nous fait nos forces recueillir
Et toujours frais en ses combats fait estre:

Mais ce n'est pas qu'en rien nous favorise,
Cil qui les Dieus et les hommes mesprise:
Mais pour plus fort contre les fors paroitre.

Here is a translation in modern English of the surface text:

Since cruel Love first poisoned my breast with his fire, I have been burning with his divine fury. It has not left me one single day.

No matter how many tasks I have undertaken – and he has given me many – no matter how much I have experienced threat and imminent ruin, no matter how impressed I have been by the power of death to end everything, my burning heart has never felt surprised by the continuing onslaught.

The more Love attacks us, the more he compels us to redouble our forces to retaliate.

This is not because he, who despises both men and Gods, is trying to help us in any way; it is simply to show off his strength in combat with the strong.

The content of this sonnet can be rephrased in a more modern idiom so that the personal reflection of the subject on her condition emerges:

> Since I first fell in love, my obsession has never left me. My feelings were so intense that nothing surprised me any more.
>
> Even the thought of the ultimate ending of all in death, even the awareness of the risks I was taking, had no effect on me.
>
> No matter how strongly love affects us, we somehow choose to involve ourselves with it increasingly.
>
> This does not mean that we think we have any inbuilt resistance to its devastating effects, but it goes to show that this emotional factor is powerful enough to undermine any human purpose, no matter how much the individual is determined to come to terms with it.

The principal adjustment I have made in rephrasing, is to replace the personification of love – Amour – with a reference to an inner factor in the subject's psychological make-up. This clarifies the awareness of a specific state of distress. The substitution of more familiar terminology makes the division between the lover's initial account of her experience, and the subsequent reflection upon it, stand out more clearly. The first eight lines portray vividly a state of mind from which the lover can find no re lease. The subsequent sestet offers a different perspective; it presents the problem from a universal viewpoint, showing it as an example of the flawed human condition, which perpetrates its own distress through its inability to rise above itself. The satisfaction of the concluding sestet lies not in a resolution of the problem, but in the poet's ability to identify the initial empirical dimension as an aspect of the basic, recognisable quandary of the human condition. It is a diagnosis, not a cure.

Although all the sonnets in this cycle are presented as aspects of a personal experience, in the final sonnet, Louise specifically addresses the other ladies of Lyons.

XXIV

Ne reprenez, Dames, si j'ay aymé:
Si j'ay senti mile torches ardentes
Mile travaus, mile douleurs mordentes:
Si en pleurant, j'ay mon tems consumé,

Las que mon nom n'en soit par vous blamé.
Si j'ay failli, les peines sont presentes,
N'aigrissez point leurs pointes violentes:
Mais estimez qu'Amour, a point nommé,

Sans votre ardeur d'un Vulcan excuser,
Sans la beauté d'Adonis acuser,
Pourra, s'il veut, plus vous rendre amoureuses:

En ayant moins que moy d'ocasion
Et plus d'estrange et forte passion.
Et gardez vous d'estre plus malheureuses.

Do not reproach me, ladies, because I have loved, because I have suffered the burning of a thousand blazing torches, a thousand labours, a thousand searing pains; if I have consumed my time in crying.

91

Alas, may my name not be condemned by you for this. If I have
blundered, I now bear the punishments; do not sharpen their harsh
points,

but realise that Love, at any given moment, without giving you the
excuse of the ardour of a Vulcan, nor the beauty of an Adonis, can,
if he chooses, cause you to be in love:

with even less opportunity than I have, and with an even greater
alienating and overwhelming passion. And take care not to be even
more unhappy than I have been.

This sonnet provides a telling account of the inevitable vulnerability of the human condition, which it is pointless to deny. She
tells other women not to mock her for writing of her susceptibility,
nor for admitting to the distress it has caused her. She reminds
them that they too are human, and therefore just as likely as she to
become victims of this affliction. Moreover, it will not be force of
circumstance which causes their involvement in this wretched state
of affairs, or the beauty and ardour of any particular man, but their
own inevitably blighted humanity.

Louise's sonnets are in no sense conceived as a poeticised plaint.
They express an ironic clear-sightedness of a recognisable state of
mind. In them, we see the lover as a conscious victim of her plight
who, by the sheer intensity of her response to its relentless impact,
ironically refuels it. After reading the *Débat*, it is apparent that
Louise had no illusions about the vulnerability of humanity. The
fact that she so skilfully found images and conceits to illustrate the
wretchedness that human beings inevitably encounter, makes these
quandaries aesthetically acceptable, even if the actual experience
they describe, more often than not, defies articulation. Her work

4. *The Idiom of Folly*

is unique in charting the point of encounter between of the creation of an emotively stimulating poetry, and the challenge presented by love to the stability of the human condition.

5

Shakespeare's Tenth Muse
Ecstasy and Melancholy in the Sonnets

Shakespeare's sonnets were first published in 1609, but known before then. They were cited in a catalogue of 1598 as 'his sugar'd sonnets among his private friends'. Today, even the best known of the sonnets remain in many ways obscure. To whom were they addressed? Who was the dark lady? Who was the beautiful youth? Do the recurrent references to the youth suggest homosexuality in Shakespeare's life? Such questions have not helped to reveal the true genius of the sonnets. This becomes more apparent when they are seen from a perspective drawn from prior European culture. When they are read with an understanding of the identity of the poet as it had evolved in Italy and France, Shakespeare's sonnets display a substantial achievement. By drawing on elements in Renaissance culture, and by dismissing stale, imitative, techniques, Shakespeare was able to make of the sonnet a vehicle to convey both the ecstasy and the melancholy of human experience. The sonnets portray the human spirit as alternately galvanised by love, degraded by sexual obsession and mercilessly threatened by time, age and decay. These considerations are implicit throughout the collection, enhancing one another.

In order to understand how Shakespeare revised the concept of the sonnet, it is useful reconsider the European climate in the sixteenth century. Ronsard's *Amours* and some of the writings of Louise Labé reveal tensions in how the identity of the poet was understood. As I have suggested, Ronsard was indebted to Ficino's commentaries on Plato. Ficino's interpretation of the *Symposium*, which describes love making order out of chaos, and of the *Phaedrus*, in which the poet and lover are portrayed as enlightened by a divine fury, were plundered by the poets of the *Pléiade*. These ideas lent a status to the poets of the Pléiade, and implicitly a divine quality to their poetry, including their love poetry. Louise's *Débat de Folie et d'Amour*, on the other hand, ridicules the state of mind of the lover, showing the effect of love to be deluded and disorientating. It draws on the ironic stance of Lucianic satire to challenge the neo-Platonic myth that the creative power of love leads men to live altruistically, contrasting this ideal with the blunt reality of human inadequacy. This contrast could, of course, be ascribed merely to a difference in genre. However, Louise's own sonnets indicate that she laments the human susceptibility to love, and finds its inevitable effects compromising.

Shakespeare's sonnets combine both perspectives of love. They demonstrate love as an exhilarating experience, leading to a positive perspective of life. On the other hand, they also show the bleakness of human inadequacy, and the melancholy which the elation disguises. This duality is apparent in *A Midsummer Night's Dream*, presumably written around the same time as the sonnets, in the early 1590s. Shakespeare drew this play from a creative fascination with the irrational and obsessive effects of love. Although the several lovers are ultimately content with their lot, this is only because the charm that induced Demetrius to fall in

love with Helena was allowed to retain its effect, thus adjusting the
initial rancour and jealousy which had beset poor unloved Helena.
Theseus, in his palace, offers this lordly comment towards the end
of the play:

> I never may believe
> These antique fables nor these fairy toys.
> Lovers and madmen have such seething brains,
> Such shaping fantasies, that apprehend
> More than cool reason ever comprehends.
> The lunatic, the lover and the poet
> Are of imagination all compact:
> One sees more devils than vast Hell can hold –
> That is the madman: the lover, all as frantic,
> Sees Helen's beauty in a brow of Egypt:
> The poet's eye, in a fine frenzy rolling,
> Doth glance from heaven to earth, from earth to heaven;
> And, as imagination bodies forth,
> The forms of things unknown, the poet's pen
> Turns them to shape, and gives to airy nothing
> A local habitation and a name. (V. 1. 1-18)

Hippolyta, however, insists that the resolution of the lovers'
quandary and their mutual bliss indicate something of ultimate
value, beyond the madness of which Theseus speaks:

> ... all their minds transfigured so together,
> More witnesseth than fancy's images,
> And grows to something of great constancy;
> But, howsoever, strange and admirable. (V. i. 24-27)

This appreciation of the duality of the lover's insight, part delusion, part enlightenment, lies at the heart of the sonnets. In order to present the positive element of this duality, it would seem that Shakespeare drew directly on Plato's *Phaedrus*. In this dialogue, Socrates presents the inspiration of love as a privileged insight: a lens through which to perceive the essentially positive features of existence. Plato's texts were widely available in sixteenth-century Europe in Latin translation. The commentaries of Ficino had helped to make the dialogues accessible to contemporary readers in Italy and France, by blending them with Christianity, but Ficino's version was adjusted to obscure what might have been seen as homosexual elements in the dialogues, and to present Plato's thought as more compatible with Christianity. Shakespeare read the Latin translation of the *Phaedrus*, unaffected by Ficino's commentaries. In the *Phaedrus*, Plato records that Socrates expounded the notion that the soul, incarnated in the human body, will strive to return to a higher plane of truth. In the course of striving, the soul is imbued with a kind of madness. Lovers, philosophers and poets, the *Phaedrus* states, have souls which particularly long to reach a higher order, and display a form of maniac possession. This was mentioned in Ficino's version and was much drawn on by the poets of the *Pléiade* to establish the spiritual independence of the poet, and to free him from servility to a patron's whim.

However, one feature of the *Phaedrus* was clearly incompatible with sixteenth-century Christianity. This was the homosexual dimension of love, so prominent in the Socratic dialogues. This was deliberately obscured by Ficino. An important feature of the *Phaedrus* was Socrates' recommendation to the soul that pursued truth, that it could be inspired to seek a higher truth through an ecstatic response to a beautiful young man. The young man of Shakespeare's sonnets perhaps come from here. The young man whom the sonnets evoke becomes an image which draws the perception of the lover toward all that is essentially good and true.

The terms used in the *Phaedrus*, moreover, cohere very plausibly with the description of the lover's anguish as established by Petrarch. The soul of the lover is said by Socrates to be reminded of divine truth by the beauty of his lover, and to be thus encouraged into a state of ecstatic longing. This state is described as a mixture of pleasure and pain. The sufferer is perplexed by the strangeness of his experience, and struggles helplessly, unable to sleep at night or to remain still by day. This condition, Socrates observes, can damage the soul's involvement with social responsibilities and family loyalties might well be abandoned. (Louise's *Débat* will be recalled here, for Mercury's dismissive comments on women forgetting their family responsibilities through the effects of love.) However, the soul can be inspired by its love to associate its response to the beloved with a search for wisdom and truth.

Shakespeare's dynamic mind saw how these ideas could provide a licence to expand the scope of the sonnet beyond a lament of the lover's woes to a celebration of a galvanised response to the most positive features of life. The lover's mind, described by Socrates in the *Phaedrus* as possessed by a frenzy of passion for the young man, is not subject to any imposition of reason. Indeed, as Socrates says, because he stands apart from the common objects of human ambition and applies himself to the divine, he is reproached by most men for being out of his wits; they do not realise that he is in fact possessed by a god. His words can be read as endemically distorted by a lack of reason, and therefore dismissed. On the other hand, a voice unaffected by preconceptions and by social status has a freedom to form the most riveting responses to life.

The persona of Shakespeare's sonnets thus presents three levels of comment. Memorably he presents the perspective of the lover's world, in which love alone is the criterion of truth. The sonnets addressed to the young man are framed with this concept in mind. On the other hand, a bleaker presentation of human experience is often presented as well. The licence Shakespeare drew from the *Phaedrus* according to which he could offer a view of a life inspired by adoration for the beloved, also offered the scope to depict a world imbued with unremitting bleakness. The description in the *Phaedrus* of the lover's passion shows it as a mere stage on the way to a perception of truth. The truth of a world *without* joy is transparent in many of Shakespeare's sonnets. This perception is drawn from the melancholy which prevails in the absence of the young man. When the uninspired soul contemplates its bereft condition, life is simply bleak. Shakespeare's sonnets, therefore, contain an implicit commentary on the quandary of the human condition. The poetic account of love had in the immediate past been codified by the overworked Petrarchan legacy, which provided a term for every aspect of love, thus leaving any depiction of the actual experience more remote. Shakespeare took the depiction of love on to a more subjective plane, where experience primes the expression of the inspiration of the young man and also the dereliction of his absence.

The figure of the young man perhaps seemed startling at the time the sonnets were written, but it was essential for Shakespeare's purpose. It enabled him to present the insights of love as related to a love of life, and not simply the result of a sexual addiction. The borrowing of the figure of the young man from the

Phaedrus allowed a clean break from mourning the wretchedness of sexual vulnerability, as Petrarch had done. The young man leads the persona of the sonnets towards an apprehension of what is intrinsically valuable. However, the persona created in the sonnets is not shown as exclusively enlightened by love for the young man. In his absence, the persona is portrayed as a victim of the human condition. Shakespeare apparently shared with the French essayist Montaigne an awareness of man's readiness to delude himself about the adequacy of his perceptions, when these in fact are relative. In some sonnets, the persona is able to build a truth which starts and ends with his commitment to his passion for the youth. These poems are exuberant. However, he is just as able to present a world which only the distraction of his fancy makes bearable. The duality of this persona enables Shakespeare to abandon any rigorously sustained perspective, which might well have been artificial and reductive. The range of the sonnets from effervescent delight to melancholy thus becomes the token of their humanity.

Perhaps the most famous sonnet is 116, which can be read as an act of faith. It is addressed to no one, but reads as a commitment to the ability of the mind to link with another without hindrance.

> Let me not to the marriage of true minds
> Admit impediments; love is not love
> Which alters when it alteration finds,
> Or bends with the remover to remove.
> O no, it is an ever fixed mark
> That looks on tempests and is never shaken;
> It is the star to ev'ry wandering bark,
> Whose worth's unknown, although his height be taken.
> Love's not Time's fool, though rosy lips and cheeks

Within his bending sickle's compass come,
Love alters not with his brief hours and weeks,
But bears it out even to the edge of doom:
If this be error and upon me proved,
I never writ, nor no man ever loved.

This may easily be understood as a statement embodying emotional truth, and one to which the persona of the sonnets would appear to subscribe unremittingly. However, the image of the star alone suggests some limitation to the absolute quality of the idea. In tribute to the wisdom of contemporary astronomers, Shakespeare comments that its height is taken. Its value to the mariner's need of direction is unquestioned. But, beyond its fulfilment of this human need, its 'worth' is not known. At the heart of this image there is mystery. The last two lines indicate clearly that the terms of the truth of this sonnet are valid within the compass of writing and of loving alone. In the process of loving and of creating poetry, according to the *Phaedrus*, the soul is drawn away from a worldly concept of reality. It is described thus in the *Phaedrus*:

> Such a process is simply the recollection of the things which our soul once perceived when it took its journey to a god, looking down from above to those things to which we now ascribe reality and gazing upwards to what is truly real. (34)

The analogy with the process described in the *Phaedrus* allows this poem to stand as a truth in terms other than the worldly. It thus acquires dignity.

However, the very scepticism that prompted Shakespeare to present an ecstatic tribute to love in the sonnets as a different side to the same coin is the result of his acknowledgement of the heavy, earthbound reality of the human condition. This awareness is a recurrent feature of the sonnets, and is markedly present when his muse, the fair youth, vanishes from them. In Sonnet 44, the lover asserts that the very lack of his ability to transcend his earthbound humanity is the cause of his affliction:

> If the dull substance of my flesh were thought,
> Injurious distance should not stop my way,
> For then despite of space I would be brought
> From limits far remote, where thou dost stay.
> No matter then, although my foot did stand
> Upon the farthest earth removed from thee,
> For nimble thought can jump both sea and land,
> As soon as think the place where he would be.
> But ah, thought kills me that I am not thought
> To leap large lengths of miles when thou art gone,
> But that so much of earth and water wrought
> I must attend time's leisure with my moan.
> > Receiving naught by elements so slow,
> > But heavy tears, badges of either's woe.

This is a statement of the physical frustration of the human condition, epitomised by the cry, 'But ah, thought kills me that I am not thought.' The acknowledgement of the essential imperfection of life comes as a striking contrast to the ecstatic commitment to the 'truth' of the marriage of true minds, to which the lover would allow no obstacle.

The following sonnet links the beloved youth with air and fire, the elements thought to counteract the earth and water of melancholy, referred to in Sonnet 44:

45

The other two, slight air, and purging fire,
Are both with thee, wherever I abide,
The first my thought, the other my desire,
These present-absent with swift motion slide.
For when these quicker elements are gone
In tender embassy of love to thee
My life, being made of four, with two alone.
Sinks down to death, oppressed with melancholy;
Until life's composition be recured,
By those swift messengers returned from thee,
Who even but now come back again, assured
Of thy fair health, recounting it to me.
This told, I joy, but then no longer glad.
I send them back again, and straight grow sad.

The association of the inspiration of the youth with the lover's thought and desire indicates how specifically Shakespeare identifies the young man addressed in his sonnets with the very forces that prompt the positive content of his poems. When thought and desire are gone, 'in tender embassy of love to thee', all that remains 'sinks down to death, oppressed with melancholy'. This succinct division is illuminating. The writer of the Renaissance was aware that Aristotle saw melancholy as the other side of genius. We find in his *Opera* the following statement: 'when the melancholy humour is heated by sanguine vapours it excites a kind of holy *furor* called enthusiasm, bringing out unusual effects in philosophy, poetry and prophecy, so that something divine seems to come forth.' (1, 3)

In these sonnets, Shakespeare also draws on the inspiration of the youth's beauty to rewrite life in terms which make his love the grammar of his thought. These would quite probably be seen as the 'unusual effects' of genius. Ironically, Shakespeare challenges this sleight of hand himself, within his sonnets. His mixture of melancholy with genius draws forth the very forces which undermine the predominance of love. Shakespeare made it very clear that he could identify these forces with the riveting realism of melancholy. For example a consciousness of the erosion of life by time is a motivating theme of the sonnets. In the first seventeen sonnets, the poet envisages the effect that time will have on the youth's beauty. The images of 'winter's ragged hand' defacing him, of 'forty winters digging deep trenches in his beauty's field' bring to the reader a consciousness of this effect as powerfully as Ronsard's '*Quand vous seres bien* vieille' evokes the image of Hélène as an old woman. However, the impact, is very different. The youth is not urged to 'pluck the day', but to have a child. This surprising exhortation has been linked to the possibility of Shakespeare's designing the sonnets for the Earl of Southampton, shortly to be married. But the notion of procreation as extending human life with a kind of immortality is present, for example, in Gargantua's letter to his son in Rabelais's *Pantagruel*, in which he writes:

> ... when, at the will of Him who rules and governs all things, my soul shall leave `this mortal habitation, I shall not now account myself to be absolutely dying, but to be passing from one place to another, since in you and by you I shall remain in visible form here in this world. (*Pant.* 8)

The urging of the youth to have a son, moreover, is reminiscent of the Platonic notion of the inheritance of the soul. It forms an impressive counterbalance to the recognition of the ravages of time, perhaps especially so to Shakespeare himself who lost his only son in 1592, at around the time the sonnets were written. The concept of begetting a son is thus offered as a means of rebuffing time's tyranny, and also as an incentive to resist the temptation of assuming the permanence of existence:

> O that you were yourself, but love you are
> No longer yours, than you yourself here live. (13, 1-2)

The poet underlines the difference between the perception of life from within, and from the outside:

> Herein lives wisdom, beauty and increase;
> Without this: folly, age and cold decay. (11, 5-6)

The delusion of assuming the eternity of the present moment of consciousness is not only a feature of the poet's warning to the youth. He acknowledges it as a fallacy to which he is vulnerable as a poet:

> Then the conceit of this inconstant stay
> Sets you most rich in youth before my sight,
> Where wasteful time debateth with decay
> To change your day of youth to sullied night,
> And all at war with Time for love of you
> As he takes from you, I engraft you new. (15, 9-14)

From this point, the poet seems to show how his poetry seeks to protract the 'conceit of this inconstant stay'. This marks a turning point. Previously, he has conceded that his poetry will not have the same power to endow permanence as would the engendering of a son. In Sonnet 17, for instance, he emphasises the deficient strengths of writing:

> If I could write the beauty of your eyes
> And in fresh numbers number all your graces
> The age to come would say this Poet lies. (17, 5-7)

He adds that all he has written would be dismissed as 'a Poet's rage'.

In the following sonnet, however, the ecstatic movement toward transcending the melancholic perspective of human limitation prompts the poet to claim that his beloved's beauty exceeds that of a summer's day and that through his art the poet can endow him with 'eternal summer'.

18

Shall I compare thee to a summer's day?
Thou art more lovely and more temperate.
Rough winds do shake the darling buds of Ma,
And summer's lease hath all too short a date.
Sometimes too hot the eye of heaven shines,
And often is his gold complexion dimmed;
And evey fair from fair sometimes declines,
By chance or nature's changing course untrimmed.
But thy eterna; summer shall not fade
Nor lose possession of that fair thou ow'st.
Nor shall Death brag thou wand'rest in his shade,
When in eternal lines to time thou grow'st.
So long as men can breathe or eyes can see,
So long lives this, and this gives life to thee.

The wonder of the young man's existence will thus last as long as the poet's sonnet is spoken or read. The promise that writing can convey eternal youth to his beloved is as exuberant as the expression of admiration for his beauty. The passion for writing is therefore conceived as on the same level as his passion for the youth. Writing, moreover, is a concept thus allied to response to beauty. It is part of the pursuit of the good and true.

Other sonnets reveal a world which is spiritually dead. Sonnet 15 (in which the poet later speaks of being 'all at war with time') presents a vista of human life from a hypothetical vantage voint beyond it. The sonnet indicates a sense of life's shrunken irrelevance.

> When I consider everything that grows
> Holds in perfection but a little moment,
> That this huge stage presenteth nought but shows
> Whereon the Stars in secret influence comment;
> When I perceive that men as plants increase,
> Cheered and checked even by the selfsame sky,
> Vaunt of their youthful sap, at height decrease,
> And wear their brave state out of memory;
> Then the conceit of this inconstant stay
> Sets you most rich in youth before my sight,
> Where wasteful Time debateth with Decay
> To change your day of youth to sullied night:
> Then all in war with Time for love of you
> As he takes from you, I engraft anew.

The bleak prospect of existence here seems to fire the poet to write of the beauty of his beloved, as though he had decided to 'take arms against a sea of troubles' racked with a confusion similar to Hamlet's. Yet, in this portion of the sonnet sequence, he still urges the youth to draw his life 'from his own sweet skill' (16, 11) – presumably by having a child, which will prove 'means more blessed than my barren rhyme'.

From this point onward, the sonnets are balanced between an insight into the misery of the human condition and the essential refocusing through love of the beautiful youth which fuels his appetite to 'make war' on Time. The poet addresses Time, seeing it as all-powerful.

> Devouring Time, blunt thou the Lion's paws,
> And make the earth devour her own sweet brood,
> Pluck the keen teeth from the fierce Tiger's jaws
> And burn the long-liv'd Phoenix in her blood (19)

In his passionate fury, he defies Time to 'carve his love's fair brow' and presents this challenge as though addressed to a rival poet, or artist.

> ... draw no lines there with thine antique pen (19, 10)

The sonnet ends with the bland conceit that whatever Time may do, the young man shall in the poet's verse 'ever live young'. The impact of the sonnet lies in the implicit acknowledgement of the helpless vulnerability of all life. And yet such acknowledgement provides the most passionate incentive to write.

The capacity to write poetry embodies in the sonnets an empowering ecstasy as much as does the passionate response to the beauty of the young man. Perhaps they are one and the same. Sonnet 23 compares stage fright with the lover's fears:

> As an unperfect actor on the stage
> Who with his fear is put beside his part
> Or some fierce thing replete with too much rage,
> Whose strength's abundance weakens his own heart,
> So I for fear of trust, forget to say
> The perfect ceremony of love's rite,
> And in mine own love's strength seem to decay (1-7)

These very human analogies with a basic sense of incompetence and lack of resource encourage empathy from the reader in terms of a human experience drawn from a flaw in professional confidence. Further on, the plea is made to 'let his books be his eloquence':

> O learn to read what silent love hath writ
> To hear with eyes belongs to love's fine wit. (13-14)

His poetry is seen as empowering him, in a way that transcends his essential deficiencies.

Sonnets 25 and 29 present human existence in a deeply sceptical way. In 25 the perspective is social. It portrays a world in which there is no stability, and in which each man depends exclusively on the whim of the favour of the powerful for his identity:

> Great Prince's favourites their fair leaves spread
> But as the marigold at the sun's eye,
> And in themselves their pride lies buried

For at a frown they in their glory die.
The painful warrior, famoused for worth,
After a thousand victories once foil'd,
Is from the book of honour razed forth,
And all the rest forgot for which he toil'd. (5-12)

The final couplet flippantly celebrates the relative security of love, which, it is claimed, is not subject to such vagaries.

Then happy I that love and am beloved
Where I may not remove nor be removed.

Sonnet 29 presents the wretchedness of feeling at odds with society. A vivid portrait is painted here of the frustration of failure, the debilitation of jealousy, and the ultimate consequence of rejection, which leads to self-loathing:

When in disgrace with Fortune and men's eyes
I all alone beweep my outcast state
And trouble deaf heaven with my bootless cries,
And look upon myself and curse my fate,
Wishing me like to one more rich in hope
Featured like him, like him with friends possess'd,
Desiring this man's art and that man's scope,
With what I most enjoy contented least, (1-8)

The concluding couplet invokes the simplicity of that of Sonnet 25:

For thy sweet love remember'd such wealth brings
That then I scorn to change my state with kings.

Again, the 'turn' of this sonnet, in its clarity, has the power to cast a dauntingly qualifying perspective on the preceding lines.

The final sonnet I should like to consider in this section is one of the most famous: Sonnet 30, which even more than the two just discussed expresses with overwhelming sensitivity the spiral of defeat encountered in reflective thought. It demonstrates the self-destruction of the mind which follows obsessive recollection, recreating previous situations which have undermined its security:

> When to the sessions of sweet silent thought
> I summon up remembrance of things past,
> I sigh the lack of many a thing I sought
> And with old woes new wail my dear time's waste:
> Then can I drown an eye (unus'd to flow)
> For precious friends hid in death's dateless night
> And weep afresh love's long since cancell'd woe,
> And moan th'expense of many a vanish'd sight.
> Then can I grieve at grievances foregone
> And heavily from woe to woe tell o'er
> The sad account of fore-bemoaned moan
> Which I new pay, as if not paid before.
> But if the while I think of thee, dear friend,
> All losses are restor'd, and sorrows end.

This sensitive account of severe depression has the effect of presenting the ultimate thought of the beloved as a diversion which obscures the negative reality of the human predicament. Nevertheless, the body of the sonnet itself does nothing other than reinforce it. Melancholy sullies the sessions of sweet silent thought.

As the cycle progresses, the spiritual isolation of the human condition is emphasised. In Sonnet 121 there is no diversion. The interior perspective is utterly disregarded by the superficial judgement of the outer world, reminiscent of Hamlet's comment to his stepmother, 'Nay madam, 'tis. I know not seems,' when she asks him why his father's death should 'seem so particular' to him.

> 'Tis better to be vile than vile esteemed
> When not to be, receives reproach of being,
> And the just pleasure lost, which is so deemed
> Not by our feeling but by others' seeing. (1-4)

The final sonnets are the bleakest. In Sonnet 130, Shakespeare systematically demolishes the Petrarchan lexicon, beginning with 'My mistress' eyes are nothing like the sun.' Wittily, the sonnet ends with the assertion that imagery is redundant, and that the woman of whom he speaks would be as fair as any 'belied with false compare'. From this point onwards, however, neither love nor poetry manages to propel the persona of the sonnets beyond a sense of wretchedness. The switch to the 'dark lady' as addressee itself seems to announce a change of angle. The abandonment of the fair youth is significant, since at this point all allusions to the *Phaedrus* disappear.

The concluding sonnets show the effect of love on a man as confusing rather than exhilarating. Sonnet 129 speaks of lust as a force which totally undermines any integrity:

> Th'expense of Spirit in a waste of shame
> Is lust in action, and till action, lust
> Is perjur'd, murd'rous, bloody, full of blame,

Savage, extreme, rude, cruel, not to trust,
Enjoy'd no sooner but despised straight,
Past reason hunted, and no sooner had
Past reason hated as a swallowed bait,
On purpose laid to make the taker mad.
Mad in pursuit and in possession so,
Had, having, and in quest to have, extreme,
A bliss in proof, and prov'd a very woe,
Before a joy propos'd, behind a dream.
All this the world well knows, yet none knows well
To shun the heaven that leads men to this hell.

This sonnet in effect would seem to dismantle the very ethos of the love sonnet. It illustrates a state of mind obsessed with sexual passion in a totally negative way. The pursuit of the object of desire is demeaning. It is shown as robbing the mind of its independence of spirit. It is significant that the vocabulary in the final couplet has altered radically from that of the early sonnets: the poet speaks of heaven and hell. The antithesis here illustrates the human delusion as to what constitutes heaven: lust, in fact, leads to hell. In other sonnets towards the end of the cycle, the poet openly acknowledges that a love fuelled by lust alone clouds the mind. There is no longer the note of conviction which radiated a sense of a higher truth, perceptible only to a mind intoxicated by the young man:

O cunning love, with tears thou keep'st me blind,
Lest eyes well seeing thy foul faults should find (148, 13-14)

The shifting presentations of love in the sonnets imply a shifting perspective of values. This may indicate a fundamental scepticism in Shakespeare's mind. By drawing on the attraction towards the beautiful youth described by Socrates in the *Phaedrus*, he is able to confer an antique dignity on the state of mind often treated in his times as a form of sickness, or idiocy. By dismissing the stale Petrarchan lexicon, he is able to express experientially the intensity of passion. However, the idea expressed in the *Phaedrus*, that the exhilaration roused by love for the young man is a stage in the pursuit of truth, gives Shakespeare the licence to present a contrast between the ecstasy of love and the poverty of the human condition without it. This contrast links the concept of a basic melancholy with the insight of genius. The dignity which the allusion to the *Phaedrus* confers on the perspective of love saves it from a dismissive response. The bleakness of the melancholy alternative acquires increasing impetus as the cycle proceeds.

The contrast in perspective to be found in the sonnets reflects many of Shakespeare's plays. Graham Bradshaw in *Shakespeare's Skepticism* (New York, 1987) points out what he calls the 'dramatic perspectivism' of the plays:

> Just as Shakespeare exposes the terrible gap between what must be expected of life at its worst and what we customarily expect a work of art to do or not to do, he exposes the gap between different characters' intensely apprehended need for values like 'justice' and the apparent absence or invisibility of any corresponding Order or Justice in the plays' world. (93)

Recurrent in Shakespeare's drama is an open focus on the content of values. *Troilus and Cressida* perhaps offers the most striking example. 'What's aught, but as 'tis valew'd?' demands Troilus, prompting Hector's insistence on intrinsic value (*Troilus and Cressida* 2, ii):

But value dwells not in particular will,
It holds his estimate and dignitiy
As well, wherein 'tis precious of it selfe
As in the prizer:

However, Ulysses explains to Achilles in 3.iii that our minds have no reliable means of identifying the objectivity of a value. Graham Bradshaw finds here a similarity with Montaigne, when he

> ... will not deny that there may be witches or miracles, but denies that the human mind can establish the genuineness of either phenomenon. This makes the crucial difference between *dogmatic* scepticism ... and radical scepticism, which turns on itself – weighing the human need to affirm values against the inherently problematic nature of all acts of valuing. (39)

The sonnets show the mind swinging between an ecstatic response to the beauty of youthful life, and a sense of nullity when it has no such impetus. The implication is that we crave to give a meaning to existence in order to survive, however impossible it may be to credit this meaning with any objective value.

6

The Idiom of Fragmentation
John Donne

So far, all the writers discussed have been considered in terms of their relation to a literary and philosophical context. In the work of Petrarch, Ronsard, Louise Labé and Shakespeare, the biographical element is tantalising but only marginally helpful. Although fuelled with experience, the persona of their poetry is a literary self. However, the writings of John Donne would appear to reflect the tensions of his actual life, and therefore their biographical context is unavoidable.

Since its inception, the stance of the sonnet was generally subjective, if not precisely autobiograpical. This stance gave scope to interiority. It also invited the identification of the reader, who, if sufficiently enticed, would be willing to take up the invitation to endorse a particular emotional response, and then, in the event of a 'turn', to adjust this response accordingly. By drawing on this technique, the sonneteer was free to explore very many complex experiences, their challenge and, if only through wit, the possibility of some kind of resolution. Donne, however, had difficulties in drawing on the concept of the self as a literary device. The self in Donne's writing often appears ravaged. His circumstances riddled his self-awareness with emotional and spiritual problems, which find a tortured expression in his work. His love poetry is in particular affected by them. It is worthwhile to consider them in detail.

The insecurity of spiritual identity which his work suggests seems to have originated from the earliest days of his life. Donne was born a Catholic. His mother was a descendant of Thomas More. He saw members of his family persecuted for their faith. His brother Henry was imprisoned for harbouring a priest in his home. Although Donne was successful in his studies at Oxford, he did not take his degree, for his Catholic friends advised him against the necessary oath of allegiance to the spiritual authority of the throne, which would compromise his faith. He went on to study at Cambridge, but again desisted from taking his degree, for similar reasons. When his stepfather died, his mother appointed tutors to teach him mathematics and liberal studies; Donne's biographer, Izaac Walton, claims that they were 'advised to instil particular principles of the Romish Church of which those Tutors profes'd (though secretly) themselves to be members.' (Walton, *The Lives of John Donne etc.* (London, 1973) p. 14.)

Donne studied law for a time at Lincoln's Inn Fields. He was now very much in contact with a worldly society. His earliest poetry, the *Satires*, indicates a lively and energetic mind, driven by a fierce passion to destroy pretension. Much of the content of the *Satires* is ribald scoffing directed at his contemporaries; he sets himself up as a moral arbiter, rebuking the lack of authority at the Inns of Court. Even in these early works, for which he never claimed importance, it is however possible to identify the insecurity of Donne's religious stance. In Satire 3 the poet cites four fictitious characters, who describe, with much disdain, their religious affiliations. Donne's Catholic prototype, Mirreus, seeks'true religion' in Rome, since he knows that 'she was there a thousand years ago'. (47) All that remains now, says the poet, are rags. Crants, the Reformer, however, responds to what is called religion at Geneva, a faith described by the poet as:

> ... plain, simple, sullen, young,
> Contemptuous, yet unhandsome (51-52)

This is hardly an endearing characterisation of the Reformed faith; one would not guess from it that Donne, the man, as opposed to the poet / persona, is being lured towards it.

The poet's own voice, however, now intervenes with what seems to be a personal insight:

> though truth and falsehood be
> Near twins, yet truth a little elder is;
> Be busy to seek her, believe me this
> He's not of none, nor worst, that seeks the best.
> To adore, or scorn an image, or protest
> May all be bad; doubt wisely; in strange way
> To stand inquiring right, is not to stray;
> To sleep, or run wrong is. On a huge hill,
> Cragged and steep, Truth stands, and he that will
> Reach her, about must, and about must go;
> And what the hill's suddenness resists, win so;
> Yet strive so, that before age, death's twilight,
> Thy soul rest, for none can work in that light. (72-84)

Here we have evidence of Donne's determination to face honestly the conundrum of faith. Although his perspective is overtly impartial, it is clear that, like Erasmus, he trusted the human mind to identify truth when it is discovered. This confidence he would have derived from his Catholic upbringing, which taught that human reason was freely able to identify the good. The young man's view of age as 'death's twilight' (83) shows that Donne had an inner determination to come to terms with faith in order to find peace of mind.

Izaac Walton records Donne's preoccupation with religion when he was young:

> He was now entered into the eighteenth year of his age; and at that time had betrothed himself to no religion that might give him any other denomination than a *Christian*. And Reason and Piety had both perswaded him that there could be no such sin as Schisme if an adherence to some visible Church were not necessary. (25)

Such objective common sense would seem eminently reasonable and well focused to resist the unremitting tensions of his times. Yet commitment to faith was not merely a matter of intellectual speculation. Donne was aware of pressure on him to reject his Catholic background and commit himself to Anglicanism. Walton continues:

> About the nineteenth year of his age, he, being then unresolved what Religion to adhere to, and considering how much it concern'd his soul to choose the most Orthodox, did therefore (though his youth and health, promised him a long life) to rectifie all scruples that might concern that, presently lay aside all study of the Law: and, of all other Sciences which might give him a denomination; and began seriously to survey, and consider the Body of Divinity, as it was then controverted between the *Reformed* and the *Roman Church*. (25)

6. The Idiom of Fragmentation

Donne read earnestly. When later on he lived in Mitcham, Walton records that he

> ... destined some days to a study of some points of Controversie betwixt the *English* and the *Roman Church*; and especially those of *Supremacy* and *Allegiance*: and to that place and such studies he would willinglyhave wedded himself during his life. (38)

It is clear that Donne's reading formed a part of a serious personal project. He was aware that to commit himself to the Anglican Church was essential for the purpose of establishing a successful career. He was, however, also seeking an interior change from the spiritual perspective with which he had been brought up.

His satiric focus on the Catholic Church developed early. By 1610, he was ready to write a long tract, the *Pseudo Martyr*, in which he mocks Catholics for refusing to take the oath of allegiance to the king. He blames Catholics who consciously incur the death penalty for refusing to take the oath, of 'unnatural behaviour' since 'no man, by law of nature might deliver himself unto an evil which he might avoide. ' (Carey, 19) This tract won favour in the eyes of James I, who eventually persuaded him to take orders. However, for Donne to mock the spiritual integrity that drove his mother's ancestor, Thomas More, to submit himself to martyrdom must have been a hard choice. He filled *Pseudo Martyr* with scurrilous allegations against Catholics, accusing them of sexual perversion and fraud. He was pleased to vent his wrath against posture, as he had done in the *Satires*. However, on another level his stance clearly caused him pain. Some years after writing *Pseudo Martyr*, he admitted to the distress his apostasy had brought him:

121

I had a longer worke to doe than many other men; for I was first to blot out certaine impressions of the Romane religion, and to wrastle both against the examples and against the reasons, by which some hold was taken; and some anticipations early layde upon my conscience, both by persons who by nature had a powere and a superiority over my will, and others who by their learning and good life, seem'd to me justly to claime an interest for the guiding, and rectifying of mine understanding in these matters. (Carey *Life*, *Life*, *Mind and Art*, 15.)

The experiences of Donne's early years were not merely drawn from his reading, however. A relish for adventure and experience led him to join the Earl of Essex in his expedition to Cadiz, in 1593. The closeness to death which he experienced appears to have been both exhilarating and devastating. The storm broke shortly after their departure from Plymouth Donne's description of this event in his poem 'The Storm' demonstrates his readiness to interpret experience in terms of faith. He portrays the extreme conditions of the storm as a metaphor for the instability of human existence. The whole experience, moreover, is presented as an example of how little control humans have, and how soon confidence is extinguished. From such a limited, perilous perspective, man's only surety is in faith:

> Darkness, light's elder brother, his birth-right
> Claims o'er this world, and to heaven has chased light.
> All things are one, and that one none can be,
>
> Since all forms, uniform deformity
> doth cover, so that we, except God say
> another *fiat*, shall have no more day. (67-71)

6. The Idiom of Fragmentation

After his return from the Spanish expedition with Essex, Donne found employment with Thomas Egerton, and moved into York House as his secretary. His subsequent involvement with Ann More, one of the ladies of the house, was to be another over-whelming experience in which, as in the storm, he was directly confronted by the extreme vulnerability of his condition. Walton describes this secret liaison with Ann with critical sympathy:

> Love is a flattering mischief, that hath denied aged and wise men a foresight of those evils that too often prove to be the children of that blind father, a passion that carries us to commit *Errors*; with as much ease as whirlwinds remove feathers, and begets in us an unwearied industry to the attainment of what we desire. And such an Industry did, not withstanding much watchfulness against it, bring them secretly together (I forbear to tell the manner how) and at last to a marriage too ... (25-28)

The gravity of Ann's father's displeasure at this union was soon to dawn on Donne. Sir George had him imprisoned. In an attempt to defuse his father-in-law's anger, Donne wrote to him, assuring him of his integrity. In his letter, he blames himself unremittingly:

> Sir, I acknowledge my fault to be so great as I dare scarce offer any other prayer to you on my own behalf but this, to believe this truth, that I neither had dishonest ends nor means (To Sir George More, 2 February 1602, *Donne* 87)

He assures Sir George that he 'tendered Ann more than his fortunes or his life, and would neither joy in this life nor enjoy the next, but for her'. He begs Sir George to deal with the matter:

as the persuasions of nature, reason, wisdom and Christianity shall inform you. (ibid.)

We see here that Donne does not try to mitigate the circumstances which have led him to marry Ann secretly, but asks for forgiveness, referring to his conscience which has compelled him to be honest and to admit his fault. This acceptance of his guilt, and reference to his conscience, are clearly linked to his recent Anglican thinking. And draw on a Protestant consciousness of endemic sinfulness. We find this stance echoed in a sermon Donne was to make at Lincoln's Inn in 1618, after his ordination.

> ... except we do come to say, Our sins are our own, God will never cut up that root in us, God will never blot out the memory in himself, of those sins. Nothing can make them none of ours, but the avowing of them, the confessing of them to be ours. (*Donne* 276. 161)

Already, in Donne's life, can be seen the tensions which were to form the framework of his writing. These were his awareness of man's inherent sinfulness, and of the blighted human propensity to lurch into a perspective that presents life exclusively from a selfish, subjective viewpoint. His reading of the negative theology of the Protestant Church would have instilled in him the rubric formulated by St Augustine, that in turning towards himself, man turned away from God. Without grace, Augustine asserted, man is bound to turn to wrong way. Clearly, it was not Donne's reading alone that impressed these salient truths on him. The events of his life, such as his father-in-law's fury at his clandestine marriage, showed him how easily man is ensnared by his own doomed condition.

Much of his early writing, especially his love poetry, consciously illustrates the confusion of the perspective from the self alone. Donne was aware that poetry emanating from the confusion of the self is no guide to truth. This is made clear by his remark in a letter to his friend, when he commented that poetry does not exist to state the truth, but rather to send warnings to show what the truth is not. Donne's love poetry is concerned with what truth is not. His love poetry is best read as a series of warnings. The love poetry written after 1593 is not, however, presented from an overtly satirical point of view. It is easy for the modern post-romantic reader to assume that Donne identified personally with his love poetry, and that, in writing it, Donne is retrospectively relishing in recreating his amorous experience, or self-indulgently recreating it. But, seen in the context of his overwhelming awareness of inherent sinfulness, these poems appear as an illustration of a state of mind which he knew and acknowledged, to be fallen.

In 'The Triple Fool', Donne gives a succinct summary of how love poetry indicates a moral compromise:

> I am two fools, I know,
> For loving and for saying so
> In whining poetry;
> But where's the wise man who would not be I
> If she did not me deny? (1-5)

In this poem, he spells out the therapy in the disciplining of emotional turmoil by the composition of verse:

> Then as th'earth's inward narrow crooked lanes
> Do purge sea water's fretful salt away,
> I thought, if I could draw my pains,

Through rhyme's vexation, I should them allay.
Grief brought to number cannot be so fierce,
For, he tames it, that fetters it in verse. (6-11)

This poem develops yet further its illustration of the paradox
involved both in being a lover and in writing poetry about love; the
poet says that another poet might well take up the same theme, and
by the power of his writing, please and sensitise his readers,
including, ironically, the original poet himself! This third paradox
completes the saga of the lover who has turned poet yet still remains
the victim of being both. It is notable that Donne 's thought here is
very far from Shakespeare's concept of the privileged mentality of
lover and poet. From the negative angle of Protestant theology, such
preoccupations are more a sign of being damned than being blessed.

There is no need to seek biographical references in the *Songs and
Sonnets*. Donne doubtless had relationships with women before the
one with Ann More. The state of being in love was familiar to him.
Indeed, familiarity is a deliberate and dismissive feature of his love
poetry. In 'The Indifferent', for example, he mocks himself for his
never-failing readiness to fall into his absurd pattern of response:

I can love both fair and brown,
Her whom abundance melts, and her whom want betrays,
Her who loves loneness best, and her who masks and plays,
Her whom the country formed, and whom the town,
Her who believes, and her who tries,
Her who still weeps with spongy eyes,
And her who is dry cork and never cries;
I can love her, and her, and you and you,
I can love any, so she be not true. (1-9)

6. The Idiom of Fragmentation

Donne constructed a kind of perverse lover's casuistry, which establishes its perspective from the self as the centre of the universe. His use of the idiom of love in the *Songs and Sonnets* can be fully appreciated. only through an awareness of this deliberate perversity. 'The Sun Rising' is an excellent example of this conscious egocentricity. In his playful address to the sun, the poet-persona presents the whole universe as subservient to his love-making with his mistress; indeed, they are seen to eclipse the worth of all things, undermining and excluding other values:

> She is all states, and all princes, I,
> Nothing else is.
> Princes do but play us; compared to this,
> All honour's mimic; all wealth alchemy. (21-23)

In a conversational, almost burlesque style, the poet-persona scornfully chides the sun as a busybody, who should have better things to do than to disturb him and his mistress. This sun is far different from the sun of the Petrarchan sonnet, where it was used as an image to express an absolute source of power and beauty. In Donne's poem, all such myths are belittled. Even time has no power. The fantasy of the lover is so extreme as to dismiss it entirely and reduce it to rags. Donne's familiar, iconoclastic idiom is one way of revealing love as a false absolute of corrupt human understanding.

In 'The Canonisation', the lover's casuistry is presented in liturgical language. Since Donne at this time had set his mind on the rejection of his Roman Catholic upbringing, he now finds a redundant devotional idiom shockingly appropriate to describe the inconsequential, self-destructive paradox of love. The poem begins in the same outspoken, familiar way as 'The Sun Rising':

> For god's sake, hold your tongue, and let me love.
> Or chide my palsy, or my gout,
> My five grey haires, or ruined fortune flout, (1-3)

The Petrarchan images of heat, cold, sighs, tears are in this poem summoned in the same worldly breath as litigious quarrels and recruitments of soldiers. The implication is that all matters that preoccupy humans are worthy only of cynical dismissal.

Donne then goes on to use liturgical language to talk of love. At one point, his verse reads like a mockery of Christianity, overtones of the resurrection obliquely referring to sexual excitement:

> We die and rise the same, and prove
> Mysterious by this love (26-27)

However, in the next verse he darkly indicates that love has more to do with dying than living; it is touched by mortality:

> We can die by it, if not live by love,
> And if unfit for tombs and hearse
> Our legend be, it will be fit for verse;
> And if no piece of chronicle we prove,
> We'll build in sonnets pretty rooms;
> As well as a well wrought urn becomes
> The greatest ashes, as half acre tombs,
> And by these hymns, all shall approve
> Us canonised for love. (28-36)

He presents love as a kind of self-indulgent mythology, which creates from its own impetus a form of aggrandisement of the trivial. The Roman Catholic concept of canonisation is reduced hereto the same level as self-indulgent love.

The self-destructive persona adopted in the *Songs and Sonnets* is often inferred by wit. Occasionally these poems contain an element of aphorism. Donne's ability to draw from his bleak apprehension of man's negative condition to make succinct, discerning observation, anticipates La Rochefoucauld, the famous French moralist of the later seventeenth century:

> Love is a growing, or full constant light;
> And his first minute after noon is night.
> ('Lecture upon the Shadow', 25-26)

More moving, and still marked indelibly with the helplessness and the nullity of the self, is the poem presumably written on the death of his wife, the 'Nocturnal upon Saint Lucy's Day'. In this poem, the void experienced at the loss of the beloved takes away all impetus to live. The image of the short day in which the world's sap has shrunk, indicates how love alone can provide the vitality essential for life. Its removal brings the lover to an awareness of his own essential nothingness.

> He [love] ruined me, and I am rebegot
> of absence, darkness, death, things which are not. (17-18)

He looks back on how he was able to make sense of his life (however spurious) with his lover. The lovers' predilection to see all things on the scale of love alone is reflected here:

> Oft a flood
> Have we two wept, and so
> Drowned the whole world, us two; oft did we grow
> To be two chaoses, when we did show
> Care to aught else; and often absences
> Withdrew our souls, and made us carcases. (23-27)

This poem is not to be read simply as a lament for the loss of the woman he loved. It is also a lament for the nullity of human resources. The persona of the poem is shown to have so loved his mistress (in this case, most probably his wife) that losing her means he has lost his sense of identity.

It is well known that Donne did not value his *Songs and Sonnets*. He found in them as little worth as the passionate involvement of love itself, which he portrays as essentially self-deceptive. According to Walton, he wished his poems had been 'so short liv'd that his eyes had witness'd their funerals' (Walton, 61). One might assume that for Donne to write at all was at odds with his increasing involvement with his faith. When he became ordained he forcefully disclaimed all his early interest in language and the arts. However, his private letters and meditations, – as opposed to the sermons which he would ultimately be called upon to make with a public voice, enabled him to give decisive expression to his personal experience of life. Such writing was in a totally different idiom from his love poetry. Although the *Songs and Sonnets* were charged with a fundamental rejection of all the diversion and deception love entailed, they were designed to please and to entertain in a way that later Donne, for spiritual reasons, rejected. He never so aught to publish the *Songs and Sonnets*. He came to decide that they did not constitute a valid expression of his spiritual experience, since they referred to a corrupt human perspective alone. His letters and meditations, however, do give an insight into the state of mind which developed in the light of his faith, and show how, through a harrowing consciousness of his insufficiency, he was able to verbalise what he regarded as his true experience.

A letter included in Walton's biography, indicates that a fundamental sense of what would now be called alienation possessed Donne from very early in his life. This letter was written from his home in Mitcham when he was surrounded by his wife and children.

> 'Tis now Spring, and yet all the pleasures of it displease me every other tree blossoms, and wither: I grow older and not better; my strength diminishes and my load grows heavier; and yet I would fain be or do something; but, that I cannot tell what is no wonder in this time of my sadness; for to chuse is to do; but to be no part of any body is as to be nothing; and so I am, and shall so judge my self. (37)

He goes on to recall his youthful enthusiasm for his legal studies and what he calls 'the worst voluptuousness, *an hydroptique and immoderate desire of human learning and languages*'. Now, however, he is no longer beguiled by such deceptive lures. He sees himself diminished to a nonentity.

> I am become so little, or such a nothing ... I am rather a Sickness or a Disease of the world, than any part of it, and therefore neither love it nor life ...

This stark awareness of life's fundamental bleakness appears recurrently in all Donne's later writing. It occurs in devastating form in his later *Devotions upon Emergent Occasions*, written in his illness in 1623. Here he shows himself as the agent of his own destruction, describing the very process of life as wilfully debilitating:

> Fevers upon wilful distempers of drink and surfeits, consumptions upon intemperances and licentiousness, madness upon misplacing or overbending our natural faculties, proceed from ourselves, and so that ourselves are in the plot, and we are not only passive but active too in our destruction. But what have I done, either to breathe or to breed these vapours? they tell me it is my melancholy; did I infuse, did I drink in melancholy into myself? It is my thoughtfulness; was I not made to think? (*Devotions upon Emergent Occasions*, 339, X11)

A letter written much earlier than this, to Sir Henry Goodyer in 1608, pinpoints the lacerating problem that troubles Donne; he cannot distance himself from his corruption sufficiently to remedy it.

> Of the diseases of the mind there is no criterion, no canon, no rule, for our own taste and apprehension and interpretation should be the judge, and that is the disease itself. (Letter to Sir Henry Goodyer, 156)

Donne seems to be recording here his innermost thoughts. In doing so, he realises in the same way as will the seventeenth-century Jansenist writer Pascal that the best function of reason is to demolish reason. Man can use this faculty to spell out for himself his own adequacy.

Donne's sermons are didactic; his consciousness of his listeners is greater than his self-consciousness. There is no doubt as to the authenticity of his endorsement of the theological perspective presented in them. But they were designed to make an impression on the hearer, for his or her spiritual enlightenment. They are public oratory. However In his divine poetry, Donne delves personally into the distress which his scrupulously cultivated consciousness of his condition has engendered. He discovered that poetry, and particularly the sonnet form, is a valid idiom for its expression. The divine poetry shows him entering into dialogue with God. Socrates described thought as a dialogue one has with oneself. It is clear that the only authentic dialogue Donne thought possible was with God. Only by conceiving himself from the viewpoint of God could his concept of self have any validity.

Izaac Walton emphasises the value Donne placed on his divine poetry. He did not reject it, as he had his earlier work.

He was not so fallen out with heavenly Poetry as to forsake that: no, not in his declining age; witnessed then by many Divine Sonnets, and other high, holy and harmonious Composures. (Walton, 61)

The Holy Sonnets express experientially Donne's relationship with God. Instead of the facetious construct of his love poetry, which mockingly placed the self at the centre of the world, we find here a taut structure held in place by both a force from within and by a force from beyond. The Holy Sonnets emerge from the call of the wretchedness of the self in need of grace. Unable to find worth or consistency in his own resources, the self/persona in these sonnets calls on God to crush all his mistaken self confidence and begs grace to transcend his human corruption. The impact of some of these sonnets come from Donne's ability to portray a frenzied state of mind, overwhelmed by the peril in which it finds itself.

The self-destructive pattern of consciousness of spiritual plight reveals how he can find no consistency even in his devotion. There is no aspect of his living being which is not irrevocably damaged:

Holy Sonnet 19

Oh, to vex me, contraries meet in one:
Inconstancy unnaturally hath begot
A constant habit: that when I would not
I change in vows, and in devotion.
As humorous is my contrition
As my profane love, and as soon forgot:
As riddlingly distempered, cold and hot,
As praying, as mute; as infinite, as none.
I durst not view heaven yesterday; and today
In prayers, and flattering speeches I court God:
Tomorrow I quake with true fear of his rod.
So my devout fits come and go away
Like a fantastic ague: save that here
Those are my best days, when I shake with fear

Interestingly, Donne draws on the traditional Petrarchan description of the physical experience of 'profane love' described as cold, hot, riddlingly distempered, and shows this condition without glamour. Far from separating the persona of the Holy Sonnets from that of his love poetry, he shows how the same sickness afflicts them both. But the turn of The Holy Sonnets, which finds its orbit from the axis of God's love, expresses a recognition of this sickness, and a need for help. The human condition is acknowledged as merely wretchedness, symptomatic of the treacherous instability of sin. There is no help other than grace. Even to 'court God' holds no dignity; such a demeanour would suggest confidence in the efficacy and acceptability of human manners. A state of fear alone is appropriate to face God.

Two of Donne's divine poems directly establish a relationship between human circumstances and divine insight. The experience of suffering can serve to enlighten. These poems show how it is possible to gain understanding of the need of God, through an acknowledgement of human perversity, which is born from experience rather than merely from intellectual perception.

'Good Friday, 1613. Riding Westward' recounts Donne's journey to visit his friend Sir Edward Herbert in Montgomery Castle. This poem contains a description of the contrast between the corrupt movement of the fallen soul, which follows 'pleasure' or 'business', and the direction to which the 'soul's form', its Platonic ideal – is called. Donne's physical journey, to Montgomery Castle, is towards the west. The poem recounts how he is aware that his soul is called towards the east, where Christ died. The poem spells out how the human mind recoils from contemplation of Christ's death.

> Yet dare I almost be glad I do not see
> That spectacle of too much weight for me. (15-16)

The self is eclipsed before God; knowledge of God therefore entails a rejection of all personal resources. The sight of Christ suffering in all his humanity brings home the extent of his sacrifice:

> Who sees God's face, that is self life, must die
> What a death were it then to see God die? (17-18)

135

Donne makes of his journey westward an image of his human will, turned towards itself but within the scope of God's gaze. The poem ends with a plea for the grace which will punish his will enslaved to sin, so that he will be at last fit to turn towards God:

> Though these things as I ride, be from mine eye,
> They are present yet unto my memory,
> For that looks towards them; and thou look'st towards me,
> O, Saviour, as thou hang'st upon the tree;
> I turn my back to thee, but to receive
> Correction, till thy mercies bid thee leave.
> O think me worth thine anger, punish me,
> Burn off my rusts, and my deformity
> Restore thine image, so much, by thy grace,
> That thou mayst know me, and I'll turn my face (34-42)

This poem is remarkable inasmuch as it invokes the writer in the context of his worldly business, fully aware that the spiritual dimension he needs is lacking here. His chained will compels him to pursue the worldly path, and yet his memory is full of the spiritual reality of Christ's death, on which he needs to focus. We witness his plea to God to be thought worthy of chastisement so that suffering will refine him. It is clear that closeness to God is bought at a high price, which involves the rejection of all worldly affiliations, and even a plea for the imposition of suffering.

A similar perspective is to be found in the sonnet written on the death of his wife. Here the poet conveys the acceptance of the paying of his wife's debt to nature. Although he confesses that her death takes away his 'good', he recognises that she gave him the impetus to seek God. He forces himself in the midst of his distress to realise that God is showing him a love which extends beyond attachment to the physical, and that the suffering he now experiences is a refining process, which will eventually bring him close to God. God in his 'tender jealousy' needs still to strive lest the demands of the flesh, or other diabolic forces, exclude the spiritual truth so essential to the soul.

Holy Sonnet 17

Since she whom I loved hath paid her last debt
To nature, and to hers, and my good is dead,
And her soul early into heaven ravished,
Wholly on heavenly things my mind is set.
Here the admiring her my mind did whet
To seek thee God; so streams do show their head;
But though I have found thee, and thou my thirst has fed,
A holy thirsty dropsy melts me yet.
But why should I beg more love, when as thou
Dost woo my soul, for hers offering all thine:
And dost not only fear lest I allow
My love to saints and angels, things divine,
But in thy tender jealousy dost doubt
Lest the world, flesh, yea Devil put thee out.

It is fascinating that Donne, so ready to reject any facet of his own existence and any product of his creation, acknowledged the value of his Holy Sonnets. It is clear that he saw them as a true reflection of the tensions of his condition. As well as providing an expression of the tortured imprisonment of the soul by sin, they reflect the antithesis of this, which is an apprehension of the need of grace. Through his misery, he sees God's presence. This becomes increasingly marked, and provides a taut directive to the body of his verse. The self persona of the divine poetry is as fragmented and bereft as the deluded lover in the *Songs and Sonnets*. But now he presents himself in all consciousness of his ravaged self and shows that he is not content to placate his inadequacies with lies. Now he speaks out his desperate need for God to destroy all the human corruption in him, and heal him through grace.

The idiom used in these poems is an idiom of love although Donne is not endeavouring to 'court' God. He throws himself on God's mercy by an admission of his sinfulness, acknowledging that God's love alone can save him.

Holy Sonnet 13

Thou hast made me, and shall thy work decay?
Repair me now, for now mine end doth haste
I run to death and death meets me as fast.
And all my pleasures are like yesterday,
I dare not move my dim eyes any way,
Despair behind, and death before doth cast
Such terror, and my feebled flesh doth waste
By sin in it, which it towards hell doth weigh;
Only thou art above, and when towards thee
By thy leave I can look, I rise again;
But our old subtle foe so tempteth me,
That not one hour myself I can sustain;
Thy grace may wing me to prevent his art,
And thou like adamant draw mine iron heart.

138

6. *The Idiom of Fragmentation*

The impact of this sonnet derives from its unadorned honesty. Its imagery is drawn from the human condition itself ('dim eyes', 'feebled flesh'); but for its regular prosody, it might be a prayer.

Another startling way in which Donne presents his relationship with God is in Holy Sonnet 10, in which he uses the image of a besieged town to describe the soul's resistance to its conqueror. He shows the paradox of the soul's enslavement to the devil when it most needs to be delivered:

Holy Sonnet 10

> Batter my heart, three-person'd God, for you
> As yet but knock, breather, shine and seek to mend;
> That I may rise and stand, o'erthrow me, and bend
> Your force, to break, blow, burn, and make me new.
> I, like a usurp'sd town, to another due,
> Labour to admit you, but oh, to no end,
> Reason, your viceroy in me, me should defend,
> But is captiv'd and proves weak or untrue,
> Yet dearly I love you, and would be loved fain,
> But am betrothed unto your enemy;
> Divorce me, untie, or break that knot again,
> Take me to you, imprison me, for I
> Except you enthrall me, never shall be free,
> Nor ever chaste unless you ravish me.

The image of God as a conqueror, using his force to deliver the soul from sin, deliver deliberately supplants human values; since human concepts of freedom or chastity have no meaning on their own. Here Donne deliberately refers to the idiom of sexual love in order to show that a spiritual dimension, in other words, God's taking possession of the soul, could remove its horror and give it true value.

In Holy Sonnet 14 Donne points out the waste of distress men spend on trivial matters He regrets the states of amorous passion he has allowed himself in the past, and wishes now he could summon that emotion to a more fitting lament.

Holy Sonnet 14

O might those sighs and tears return again
Into my breast and eyes, which I have spent
That I might in this holy discontent
Mourn with some fruit, as I have mourned in vain;
In mine idolatry what showers of rain
Mine eyes did waste! What griefs my heart did rent!
That sufferance was my sin, now I repent. (1-7)

Donne's reconciliation to the writing of poetry obviously emerges from his ability to construct a form of expression compatible with his understanding of his spiritual identity. This poetry was not written to glamorise, to titillate nor to amuse. It is an honest statement of his vulnerability before God, expressed in terms of devastating personal experience.

His last poem 'A Hymn to God the Father', reads like an intimate conversation, its tone confessional and yet honestly humble.

Wilt thou forgive that sin where I begun,
Which was my sin, though it were done before;
Wilt thou forgive that sin through which I run,
And do run still though still I do deplore?

When thou hast done, thou hast not done,
For, I have more.

Wilt thou forgive that sin, which I have won
Others to sin, and made my sin their door?
Wilt thou forgive that sin which I did shun
A year or two, but wallowed in a score?
When thou hast done, thou hast not done,
For I have more.

I have a sin of fear, that when I've spun
My last thread, I shall perish on the shore;
But swear by thy self, that at my death thy Sun
Shall shine as he shines now and heretofore
And, having done that, thou hast done
I fear no more.

Walton tells how Donne arranged for this hymn to be sung to a 'grave and solemn Tune' by choristers in the Church, especially in the evening. He records Donne's words to a friend (perhaps Walton himself?) on one such occasion.

the words of this hymn have restored to me the same thoughts of joy that possest my soul in my sicknesse when I compos'd it And, O the power of Church musick! that Harmony added to this Hymn has raised the Affections of my heart, and quickened my grace of zeal and gratitude; and i observe that I always return from paying this publick duty of prayer and praise to God, with an unexpressible tranquility of mind, and a willingness to leave the world. (Walton, 62)

The Idiom of Love

The idiom of love for God in Donne's Holy Sonnets restored his fragmented self, and made a whole of his stricken writing.

7

The Dramatic Idiom
Racine

We have seen that the pivot of self is an essential feature of love poetry. It can serve either as the source of an irresolvable paradox, or as a means to lock into some overwhelming joy. Changing to a focus on the self often triggers the explosive effect of a poem. The texts so far examined contain within themselves the accumulative tensions of their ultimate impact. In each of them, the poet draws on a sense of the essential irony of the human condition, allowing him or her to angle for the response of the reader. One might say that the energy of love poetry is drawn from a confrontation with the self in which the exposure and incongruity of passion is revealed.

The idiom of love as it appears in the theatre of Jean Racine, who wrote between 1667 and 1677, differs from the poetry generated by this highly personal energy. In Racine's plays, the self takes on a different nature from the self in lyric poetry. Racine's creation is theatre. His work presents different created selves, devised by the writer to have a maximum impact on a specific audience. His writing was designed for dramatic purpose, providing for the demands of a specific cultural moment. There is thus no consistent self, as we have witnessed it in lyric poetry, in which the persona

143

of the poem is implicitly the writer, and which draws the reader into identification with the emotional conundrum of a specific situation. Racine's dramatic verse creates a series of confrontations between characters. Their projection and response are overtly to themselves and to one another. However, the dialogue is devised for dramatic purposes. The purpose is to affect the audience, and so the situation of the characters is presented obliquely. The audience virtually overhears the action of the drama and therefore its response is ultimately objective. The dramatic confrontations in Racine's theatre must therefore be appreciated as they operate within the structure of his plays. The quality of their presentation, however, inevitably contains an intimate dimension, one redolent of the tradition of lyric poetry which had, over centuries, created a climate of interior response. It is interesting to consider how Racine drew on this inheritance of the interiority of love, of its misery and dignity, in order to have an effect on an audience of the seventeenth-century.

Apart from Ronsard, the poets so far considered in this book did not seem to have a specific public in mind. They appear to have written in response to a personal need, rather than to sell copies of their work. Even Ronsard, for all his attempts to promote the innate and independent power of the poet, constantly changed the register and perspective of his work, demanding a similar agility – even metamorphosis – from his reader. At the other extreme, Donne did not appear to wish his love poetry to be read at all and cited its value as simply to illuminate falsehood. It is useful to consider Racine's theatre in contrast with the writing of his predecessors, since it was very specifically, and even commercially, projected. The factors that contributed to his design for maximum impact on audiences demonstrate how it was possible to create a

factitious emotional movement, and clinically to construct person-
alities wrestling with the effects of love. Racine's writing was
primed to have a particular effect at a particular time. An exami-
nation of his resources and how he put them to effective dramatic
purpose illustrates how the concept of love which appears in his
plays emerges from a cultural phenomenon, and not at all from
private passion.

Aristotle's *Poetics* was widely seen in seventeenth-century
France as a handbook for the guidance of playwrights. Such guidance was taken as necessary, since, from 1635, an attempt had
been underway to purify the French language, and to ensure the
linguistic and literary standard of works in French. The Académie
Française was founded for this purpose by a group of literary
friends, and, with French national prestige in view, the powerful
Cardinal Richelieu offered them his protection. The king Louis
XIII, gave his official approval. His heir, Louis XIV, became even
more involved with the cultural activity of his day. The Académie
was a source both of encouragement to writers, and – inevitably –
of censorship. This tense and febrile cultural climate led to much
lively criticism and confrontation. Records of the features of these
discussions help to form a good idea of the criteria established for
drama in seventeenth-century France, and what was being sought
by those who saw themselves as the ensurers of the quality of
production, and by their avid audiences.

The aim of the Académie Française was the purification of the
French language, and the establishment of criteria for works of art
with reference to the standards established by the Ancients.
However, playwrights and critics found much to discuss and to chal-
lenge. A famous dispute, for instance, arose about Corneille's play
Le Cid which was accused of flouting the rules of unity of time and

place and decorum established in Aristotle's *Poetics*. The seventeenth-century critic d'Aubignac published in 1657 a treatise called the *Pratique du Théatre* in which he announced that, instead of following the usual practice of referring to works of the past to illustrate his points, he would refer instead to the dramatic writing of the present day. He was interested – as the title suggests – in the *practice* of theatre rather than the theory behind it. Of all Aristotle's rules, he singled out as essential to present-day theatre the concept of *vraysemblance* (plausibility). Aristotle had written that the subject matter of drama did not necessarily have to be based on truth, but that it must *appear* to be true. He argued that it is not the function of the poet to relate what has happened, but instead what *may* happen, what is possible according to the laws of probability or necessity. This emphasis threw the reaction of the audience into a primary role. D'Aubignac wrote that if the audience were not convinced of the plausibility of a play, their interest would be lost. He criticised the playwright Corneille for spending too much time in explaining the designs and interests of his characters, so that there was little room to bring the inner workings of their hearts and minds to light.

As a result, the effectiveness of the theatre – in other words, its ability to provoke the response of the audience – was increasingly seen as a major factor in ensuring the success of a play. To know that such response was essential did not necessarily imply a grasp of the means to secure it. D'Aubignac himself thought that he understood Aristotle's principles clearly enough and wrote a play which studiously followed all the rules cited in the *Poetics*. It seems to have been a complete bore. Condé, a patron of the arts, wrote that he could not forgive Aristotle for having made d'Aubignac write such a tedious play. Clearly, following the rules alone was insufficient to ensure effective playwriting.

7. *The Dramatic Idiom*

The challenge to playwrights of the seventeenth-century was to move the audience, while keeping within the strictures imposed by the Académie. Could Aristotle be profitably followed? Could the playwright observe unity of time and place, and exclude violence from the stage, without condemning the work to boring predictability with no action? Although he was insufficiently gifted to take his own advice, d'Aubignac saw very clearly that the *action* of a play must occur within the language. 'Speech equals action, he wrote: *'Parler, c'est agir.'* Effective speech was not simply oratory, or a demonstration of eloquence. Speech must arouse emotional interest. A character in a good drama is prompted to speak, and in doing so continues to promote the overall development, and action, of the play. The effect of this speech was not only to move the drama on, but to move the audience.

Jean Racine, who began to write drama in 1667, followed d'Aubignac's comments about writing for the theatre. He possessed his own copy of the *Pratique du théâtre*. But, owing to his personal circumstances, he also possessed other resources which would ultimately establish his suitability to become a successful playwright, one supremely able to put into practice Aristotle's and d'Aubignac's observations on the primacy of audience response.

Racine had been educated at Port Royal by the Jansenists, a foundation based on the theology of St Augustine. Here, he learned the art of rhetoric, or the art of persuasion. His interest in rhetoric, moreover, apparently dated from an early age; whilst at Port Royal, he personally annotated his edition of Cicero's *De Inventione*. Above all, his studies of Ciceronian rhetoric taught him that language could produce decisive effects. The rhetorical exercises he learned demonstrated how to incur the involvement

147

of the listener, and to persuade to action. They displayed verbal action: speech specifically designed to have effect, and to maintain a psychological hold. In the course of his education, Racine copied out texts that insisted on the precedence of the development of the imagination over that of the critical faculties. Although his first encounters with rhetoric thus occurred long before he began to write for the theatre, he absorbed at an early age the link between the power of language and the response of the listener.

At Port Royal, Racine also absorbed the principles of Jansenist theology, which were to offer him a perspective on the helplessly passionate workings of the human mind. In *The City of God*, Augustine had asserted that, although man was originally created pure and perfect by God, Adam's revolt against God's will had reduced man into a sullied state of sinfulness, abominable in God's sight. Consequently, the human condition was intrinsically without merit, and no effort of man's could ever win him redemption. Blaise Pascal, also a member of the community of Port Royal in the mid-seventeenth century, wrote the fragmented work *Les Pensées* which constitutes the most famous apology for Jansenist thought, and offers a good guide to the Jansenist understanding of the human condition. *Les Pensées* prompts the reader's awareness of being the victim of his fallen state, longing for the state of peaceful perfection for which he was originally created, yet, through the consequences of original sin, helplessly lured into deceptive paths. Pascal shows man as misled by an unjustifiable self-confidence, by a desire for constant diversion, and by his passions. He asserts however that, although totally confused, man does retain a sense of his imperfection. This tragic consciousness lends him a certain nobility which lies in any willingness he might have to acknowledge his fallen condition. Pascal creates a picture of the human

148

condition. The dimensions of this picture imply Pascal's own personal involvement, as well as that of his reader. It is sufficiently comprehensive to be irrefutable. He defies his reader and himself to find any worth in man's resources, other than man's ability to recognise the truth of his condition, and urges total humility in order to prepare the soul for grace.

This account of the worthlessness of humanity – experienced from within, yet hypothetically seen from beyond – would indeed appear to be an appropriate basis for tragedy, and Racine's ability to put flesh on the arid bones of Aristotle's rules had its source in his exposure to the devastating Jansenist perception of the human condition. Aristotle's depiction in *The Poetics* of the concept of plot in drama is easily contained within the moral parameters of Jansenism. Plot for Aristotle is the artistic equivalent of action in real life. He calls the plot the first principle and the soul of a tragedy. Action, which for him is a synonym for drama, is not an *external* act, but an inward process that works outwards, thus involving the expression of the intrinsic personality of a human being. 'Plot' includes outward fortune and misfortune, but indicates especially the processes of mental life. The development of drama refers to an action which, while springing from the inward power of the will of an individual, manifests itself in external *doing*. Plot is therefore of supreme importance to the Aristotelian tragic concept. He describes tragedy as the imitation of an action which is an image of human life. To understand the poetry that Racine produced in his plays, it is essential to understand how he conceived this image, not simply in terms of deeds and incidents, but as involving the mental processes and the passionate involvements which have led to them. Tragedy was not simply a series of startling events. To attain plausibility, it must evoke a recognisable parallel in the human condition. The Jansenist view of the human condition had been made known to Racine at Port Royal, as an inescapable conundrum, containing within it demands for and the need of – absolute values but, because of its limited resources, incapable of providing them. Any action which was designed to be a convincing image of the human condition must therefore reflect this combination of aspiration and inevitable failure. Aristotle's description of the plot as the *soul* of a tragedy makes a potential theological analogy clear. Aristotle saw the relationship of the plot to a play as similar to that of the soul to the body. The play is a living organism and the plot is its moving force. When transferred to the stage, the characters through their actions and through their responses constitute the essential spiritual elements. The space in which they live and move and have their being defines the context of their projected spiritual existence.

As his audiences discovered, and discover still, the brilliance of Racine's theatre owes much to its plausibility. His plays depict situations which emerge from the implacable passionate make-up of the characters. The vicarious experience of such emotive power makes good theatre. Its exciting impact, however, does not imply plausibility. Emotional extremes might simply be pursued for sensation alone. Racine drew on his Jansenist background to find plausibility for such passion. The view of human motivation that one finds in his tragedies, and the pursuant consequences of its unbridled licence, is recognisably compatible with Jansenist theology. This is not to say that Racine was deliberately promoting Jansenism. It must be remembered that he left Port Royal before he started to write theatre. He had for some time led a contrastingly urbane existence. A reading of Racine's drama as Jansenist apologetic is quite unjustifiable. A glance at the *Traité de la Comédie* written by the Jansenist leader Pierre Nicole in 1667, indicates how the Jansenists, to the detriment of their famous pupil, saw the theatre as a source of moral depravity.

La comédie éloigne tous les remèdes qui peuvent empêcher la mauvaise impression qu'elle fait. Le coeur y est amolli par le plaisir. L'esprit y est tout occupé des objets exterieurs, et entièrement enivré des folies que l'on y voit représenter (Chap. IV)

The theatre banishes all remedies which can prevent the bad impression that it makes. The heart is softened by pleasure. The mind is occupied by external objects and is completely inebriated with the madness which is seen performed there.

Nicole's point here is that theatre inevitably *distracts* from the individual spectator's own spiritual quandary. The pleasure induced by the spectacle and by the emotions aroused by the theatre eradicates all moral awareness, and indeed opens the mind to madness. Nicole goes on to revive the medieval Church's suspicion of images, which it saw as lies:

... si toutes les choses temporelles ne sont que des figures et des ombres, en quel rang doit-on mettre les Comédies qui ne sont que les ombres des ombres. (Chap. X)

if all temporal things are but figures and shadows, on what level should one put plays which are nothing other than shadows of shadows?

Racine was distressed by this profound hostility to the theatre in his former place of nurture. Ironically, however, as a playwright, he drew the terms of his own incisive dissection of human motives, language and effects from the same perception of the human tendency to escape the truth by deliberately devised distraction.

A short consideration of his *Phèdre* will illustrate how he presents through his characters the inescapable quandary of the human condition though the language that describes their conflicting and tormented responses to themselves and to one another.

Racine called *Phèdre* his best play, saying that he hoped that his own good opinion of it would be confirmed by those who read it, and by time. Racine claimed in his preface that this play, first performed in 1677, conformed to all Aristotle's rules. He declares that Phèdre herself is drawn from Euripides, and, as Aristotle recommends, is neither entirely innocent nor entirely guilty. She is afflicted by a passion brought on by her destiny and by the anger of the gods. Her horror of her amorous addiction to her step-son reveals that it is not caused by an effort of her own will, but is a punishment sent by the gods. Racine points out that in this play there is ample distinction between vice and virtue. He says that he has decreased the evil which former play-wrights had attributed to Phèdre, by refusing to allow her to accuse her stepson of seducing her. The playwright leaves this fatal distortion of the truth to her confidante, Oenone. He appears intent in the preface on presenting his main character in a light that would suggest to the audience, the combination of pity – for Phèdre's helplessness – and terror, before the horrific force of her illegitimate passion, for which the gods would appear to be responsible. It is not, however, the moral structure outlined in the preface that creates its impressive impact. The language through which the plot is developed achieves a dimension beyond mere moral outline. The events of the play and their evolution do not alone combine to involve the audience in the full dramatic movement of the play. This is achieved by the characters' expression of their predicament. It is this magnificent expression that produces the plausibility which affects the audience.

It is through the unique motivation of his extraordinary language that we find Racine's debt to the recognisable idiom of love. Racine presents his characters in terms of their experience of themselves and of one another. However, a further dramatic element is in play: an unbridled force which prompts an acute consciousness of personal imperfection. Racine's plays show how the effect of passionate love is such that the character concerned is drawn face to face with a new experience of him or herself. The force of this passion is overwhelming, and topples any conscious effort to withstand it. The consequence is a painful consciousness of irredeemable inner conflict, in which the character is embarked, with no means of escape. The dynamism of this self-confrontation fuels the movement of the play.

Phèdre opens with a description of her given by Hippolyte's governor and confidant, Theramene, who is seeking reasons for Hippolyte's desire to leave Tréze. Phèdre has been for some time openly hostile to her stepson but now she is a sick woman, who will speak to no-one. Her subsequent appearance on the stage confirms Thérame's description of her. Her confidante, Oenone, begs her to speak and to reveal the cause of her distress. When she at last does so, the movement of the plot is underway. This is a prime example of language constituting action. Phèdre admits to her love for her stepson, an admission which constitutes in itself a statement of her tragic dilemma:

> *A peine au fils d'Egée*
> *Sous les lois de l'hymen je m'étais engagée,*
> *Mon repos, mon bonheur semblait etre affermi;*
> *Athène montra mon superbe ennemi:*
> *Je le vis, je rougis, je pâlis à sa vue;*
> *Un trouble s'éleva dans mon âme eperdue;*
> *Mes yeux ne voyaient plus, je ne pouvais parler;*
> *Je sentis tout mon corps et transir et bruler:*
> *Je reconnus Venus et se feux redoutables,*
> *D'un sang qu'elle poursuit tourments inévitables!*
>
> (1, iii, 269-277)

Hardly had I committed myself to the son of the Aegean within the laws of wedlock; My happiness appeared assured. Then Athens revealed to me my superb enemy; I saw him, I blushed, I went pale at the sight of him. Distress rose within my abandoned soul; my eyes could no longer see, I could no longer speak; all my body chilled and burned. I recognised Venus and her terrifying fires, the inevitable torments suffered by those whom she pursues.

Phèdre's account of her first meeting with Hippolyte indicates the rapidity of its effect. The images in this speech are physical; they are in fact reminiscent of Petrarch. She feels pierced with an arrow, she is on fire, her soul is lost. These images are a language which is deeply embedded in the cultural consciousness of Racine's audience; by virtue of their upbringing and education, they would have found them familiar. Phèdre is presented to the audience in terms of the intensity of her passion, of her awareness of her spiritual peril and of her recognition of forces beyond herself, which she has no ability to resist. The extremes of her state of mind are presented as inescapable. The audience is also given an alarming consciousness of her vulnerability. In disclosing her obsession, she has renounced the protection of silence. The audience is primed for a sequel in which all the areas of sensibility which her speech has revealed, will be devastatingly bombarded. The audience encounters Phèdre in terms of her own encounter with herself but in terms which have a currency and an immediacy because they have been nurtured by the tradition of the love sonnet. Through these images, Phèdre's interiority is exposed to the audience.

In the next act, Hippolyte tells Aricie, the only surviving member of a family of sworn enemies of his father, that he loves her. Initially, he comes to tell her of the freedoms he would now grant her following the news of his father's death. But the register of his speech slips quickly beyond that of politics and diplomacy; it becomes an outburst of emotional response to Aricie herself. Once more, the audience is introduced to an inner dimension of the character himself with which he professes to be unfamiliar.

> *Je vois que la raison cède a la violence.*
> *Puisque j'ai commencé de rompre le silence,*
> *Madame, il faut poursuivre; il faut vous informer*
> *D'un secret que mon coeur ne peut plus renfermer.*
> *Vous voyez devant vous un prince déplorable*
> *D'un temeraire orgeuil exemple mémorable.*
> *Moi qui, contre l'amour fierement révolté,*
> *Aux fers de ses captifs ai longtemps insulté;*
> *Qui, des faibles mortels déplorant les naufrages,*
> *Pensais toujours du bord contempler les orages;*
> *Asservi maintenant sous la commune loi,*
> *Par quel trouble me vois-je emporté loin de moi!*
> *Un moment a vaincu mon audace imprudente:*

Cette âme superbe est enfin dépendante.
Depuis plus de six mois, honteux, désespéré,
Portant partout le trait dont je suis déchiré,
Contre vous, contre moi, vainement je m'éprouve:
Présente je vous fuis; absente je vous trouve;
Dans le fond des forêts votre image me suit;
La lumiedu jour, les ombres de la nuit,
Tout retrace à mes yeux les charmes que j'évite;
Tout vous livre à l'envi le rebelle Hippolyte.
Moi- même pour tout fruit de mes soins superflus
Maintenant je me cherche et ne me trouve plus;

(2, ii, 525-548)

I have gone too far. I see that reason has given way to violence. Since I have begun to break my silence, Madam, I must continue; I must tell you a secret that my heart can no longer conceal. You see before you a pitiable prince, a memorable example of a rash pride. I, who turned proudly against love, who for so long mocked the chains of those imprisoned, who, deploring the shipwrecks of weak mortals, thought always to watch the storm from the shore – now brought down to slavery under the common law. What distress it is to see myself carried so far away from myself. One moment defeated my rash audacity. This superb soul has now lost its independence. For more than six months, shameful, desperate, always afflicted by the wound which has torn my flesh, I vainly battle against you and against myself. When you are before me, I flee from you; when you are away from me, I pursue you. In the depth of the woods, your image follows me. The light of the day, the shadows of the night, all imprint on my eyes the charms from which I fly; all deliver to you the rebellious Hippolyte. As for me, the only outcome of my futile efforts is that I seek the self I can no longer find.

7. *The Dramatic Idiom*

The images here of the chains and the shipwreck, which have become conventional since Petrarch, would have been quickly recognisable to Racine's audience. The dynamism of Hippolyte's speech arises from the conflict between his chaste pride as the warrior and the contrasting devastation of the effect of love The power of the imagery describing this state of mind is sufficiently violent to emphasise the wretchedness which its victim experiences. Love here is not an insight into possible delights; it is to Hippolyte a malevolent obsession which ravages his security. Far from cherishing the ever-present image of his beloved, Hippolyte deplores it. At the end of his outburst, Hippolyte apologises:

> *D'un coeur qui s'offre avous quel farouche entretien!*
> *Quel étrange captif pour un si beau lieu!*
> *Mais l'offrande à vos yeux en doit etre plus chère*
> *Songez que je vous parle une langue etrangère.*
>
> (2, ii, 555-558)

What wild words from a heart which offers itself to you! What a strange captive in such a lovely place! But the offering should appear even dearer to your eyes because of this. Realise that the language I now speak to you is foreign to me.

Here the effect of love is shown as strikingly negative. The traditional evocation of love as a place of beauty and the tender notion of offering the heart to the beloved are here ferociously undermined by Hippolyte's horror at the loss of his identity. He tells Aricie that the very incongruity of his obsession for her should endear him to her. The audience hears in his declaration of love, however, the irreconcilable jangling of a passion beyond control,

157

one which is fatally at odds with any sense of order or peace. Throughout this speech, it is possible to identify how Racine's dramatic gifts have enabled him to call into service his capacity to affect the audience. He has used imagery which his audience would associate with the stance of a lover, but he has blended this with evocations of confusion and fear. This presentation would inevitably have a riveting effect. The audience's familiarity with the negative view of the human condition spread by the Jansenists and the vocabulary of love, as drawn from popular lyrical poetry, created new and stimulating tensions here.

A similar contrast between the sentiments of the lover and the peril of identity which they may involve is to be found later in the play, when Phèdre confronts Hippolyte and tells him of her feelings for him. She has heard the news of her husband's death and is prompted by Oenone to see her love for her stepson as '*une flamme* ordinaire'. She seeks to confront Hippolyte, nominally to plead the cause of her own son, but soon finds herself speaking of her love for Hippolyte as she reminisces about her first encounter with Thésée, her husband. Hippolyte reacts with horror, and asks if she has forgotten that Thésée is his father and her husband. Phèdre retorts:

> *Et sur quoi jugez-vous que j'en perds la mémoire,*
> *Prince? aurais-je perdu tout le soin de ma gloire?*
> (2, v, 665-666)

And what makes you think I have forgotten this, Prince? Might I have lost all concern for my honour?

Phèdre's moral identity – her *gloire* - is evoked here to rebuff the shameful notion that she might disregard her family responsibilities. Her consciousness of the irreconcilable terms of her existence is devastating. She is propelled into an agonising description of her hatred of herself, incurred by her passionate vulnerability:

> *Eh bien ! Connais donc Phèdre et toute sa fureur.*
> *J'aime! Ne pense pas qu'au moment que je t'aime*
> *Innocente a mes yeux, je m'approuve moi-meme.*
> *Ni que du fol amour qui trouble ma raison*
> *Ma lache complaisance ait nourri le poison;*
> *Objet infortuné des vengeances célestes,*
> *Je m'abhorre encore plus que tu ne me détestes.*
>
> (2, v, 672-678)

Well then, know Phèdre in her full passion. I am in love. Do not think that as I find myself loving you I approve of myself and find myself innocent in my own eyes, or that cowardly compliance has nourished the poison of my insane love. Unfortunate object of the vengeance of the heavens, I abhor myself even more than you detest me.

Plainly she is at war with herself. She does not wait for another character to construct a hateful image of her and pour scorn on her, humiliating her for her inappropriate feelings. She does so herself. Her subsequent declaration:

> *La veuve de Thésée ose aimer Hippolyte!* (2, ii, 703)
>
> Thésée's widow dares to love Hippolyte!

is savage, and carries with it all the cruelty engendered by her own scorn of her emotional vulnerability.

159

The hideous consequences of obsessive passion move them to a different extreme: that of terror. The ability of Racine, through the persuasive art of his language, to project his characters' suffering together with the dynamic consciousness of their guilt infuses his drama with momentous and fearful action. The effect of Racine's technique is to present the impression of love as a spectacle. The audience becomes a 'voyeur'. The emotions are calculated to have an extreme effect, as they imply vulnerability and danger beyond normal experience. The audience's response leads to enjoyment of, rather than an identification with, the predicament of the characters. The power of Racine's language, in image and rhetorical trope, contributes to the plausibility of the characters. The formality of the Alexandrine distances it, controlling any risk of a deluge of overwhelming emotion. As a result, the audience is exposed to a vast expanse of passionate experience, but protected from it.

If the Jansenist moral perspective had gained a wide currency in the secular, aristocratic circles of the late seventeenth-century precisely because of its insistence on the inherent deficiencies of mankind, this gave society much scope for irony and wit. Racine created his plays for an audience with such tastes. He laid before them examples of degradation, lust and murderous jealousy, presented in terms of the Jansenist ethos which, ironically, offered protection through its familiarity.

8

Beyond Love?

We have seen that the idiom of love, as it developed through much of the poetry written between the twelfth and the seventeenth centuries, was used to speak of dimensions beyond love. Elemental human experience is raw. To be tamed, it must either be suppressed and confined within the proclaimed omniscience of an institution such as the medieval Roman Catholic Church or sifted through the conscious mind of an artist and given a new form through writing and reading.

The way in which the sonneteers of the court of Frederic II of Sicily wrote about love broke startlingly with convention. The origins of courtly love are obscure to this day; many assume it to have an Arab origin. However, the poetry of the troubadours, which first expressed courtly love in Europe, was sung. Their repetitive song described the persona / performer as repressed and defeated by his devotion to the inaccessible lady of whom he sang. The sonnet was designed for reflective reading. It did not bind reference to love by habitual and predictable phrases. Rather, its impact depended on the concept of unfettered individual experience, compelled, it seemed, to expression by the very intensity of inner feeling. Here, for the first time since classical antiquity, the individual had scope to consider his own experience, beyond the teaching of the Church.

It is therefore not surprising that the individual writer's experience of himself involved so many factors, which previously had been encompassed exclusively by theology. Inevitably, the image of himself developed by a writer of the early Middle Ages was founded in a sense of giddy abandonment; a consciousness that, by writing of his own experience, he was proclaiming a distance from a God who embodied Reason. However, the experience of which he wrote was elemental, and therefore had a reality which the writer chose not to deny, but rather to supply with an appropriate form of expression. This expression, from the early sonnets onwards, was far distant from the arid scholastic thinking of theologians. It was not constrictive. Rather, it was as dense and colourful as the experience of life. The use of imagery and the evocation of confusing, self-contradictory feelings gave these poems a content which was recognisable to the reader for its very humanity. The skill of the sonneteer in harnessing this dynamic content and guiding it through his wit and verbal dexterity, offered an ultimate sense of resolution and control, provided by the very process of thinking through an emotional problem, reliving it and often defining it memorably through writing.

Petrarch's love sonnets are famed for their imagery, which contributed to the strength of their structure. However, whereas the sonnets of Frederick II's court were essentially secular, Petrarch's are recognisably bound up with his faith. The very fact that he wrote sonnets about love in the vernacular distanced him from the Church of his time. On the other hand, his focus on the experience of being in love was not designed simply to celebrate it. His sonnets provide vivid descriptions of the state of anguish induced by love, as fastened on the mind as weals on flesh. His riveting images were weakened by his subsequent imitators. In time, they became conventions, and far removed from the dynamism which first inspired the expression of direct experience. When Petrarch first wrote the *Canzoniere* the idiom that he chose emerged as wretchedly self-deprecatory as the Confessions of St Augustine, whom he so admired. Petrarch shows amongst other things how susceptibility to the passion of love may erode all lucid response and understanding, and distract the mind from God, who, in Petrarch's eyes, alone could satisfy the soul's quest. Petrarch's sonnets do not constitute an assertion of the triumph of individual experience. Far from it. They offer an account of suffering related from the point of view of the man who experiences it.

Ronsard's love poetry is not affected by the rigours of the presence of God in his mind. Ironically, he was a priest. Yet the invigorating theme of love which would seem to inspire his sonnets is not accompanied by a sense of humiliation. It is always a vehicle to imply a personal strength. The pride in his poetic prowess which Ronsard drew from the Pléiade movement, enabled him to present, in his first collection of love sonnets, the suffering and uncertainties of love as a trial heroically endured by the lover. The precedence of his poetic role led him in the second cycle of sonnets to adjust the way in which he presented love. He now revealed a contrasting interpretation of love, this time reciprocated and enjoyed as a simple pleasure. In the last cycle addressed to Hélène, the identity of the poet himself is built up, almost at the expense of his beloved, whose flighty nature is implicitly rebuked since, unlike the gifted, seer-like poet, she is too worldly. Ronsard's aim is to expand the range of poetry itself, and so he adjusts his focus as he pleases. No forces are allowed to intervene beyond his aesthetic choice. Ronsard's ordained status may indeed have led to a lack of personal experience in amorous affairs, which would explain why the content of his sonnets is primarily poetic, yet, ironically, its brilliance lies in its power, through myth and metaphor, to convey a vital, energetic depiction of the unbridled, passionate response of sexual attraction.

It is helpful to read Louise Labé's sonnets alongside those of Ronsard. She too drew on Petrarch's imagery, and throughout her poetry runs a consciousness of her susceptibility to human failings. Because of the status of the poet established by the Ecole Lyonnaise, contemporary rivals of the Pléiade, the inherent dignity of the poet which these movements now widely proclaimed gave Louise a degree of protection from what could have been seen as a hazardous exposure of vulnerability. To proclaim an obsession with love in her sonnets was to appropriate the licence of what had hitherto in modern European literature been an exclusively male *topos*, and as such it had a pedigree. Louise's insights, however, reached beyond the pride of the renaissance poet. She was also able to link admission of the lover's vulnerability with the ironic exposure of the human condition recently delineated by Erasmus in his *Praise of Folly*. Erasmus had written from a Christian perspective, but his mind was so imbued with the styles of classical antiquity that the influence of his ironic tract virtually created a satiric climate amongst the humanists of the early sixteenth century. Because of this climate, Louise expressed in her sonnets the miseries of love, but in doing so, offered herself as an example of human folly, just as Erasmus did when, in *Praise of Folly*, he mocked scholars like himself who ruined their eyesight through reading late by candlelight. Love appears in Louise's sonnets as a feature of the human condition for which, because of its inevitability, no shame need be felt. Her sense of irony, as

164

expressed in the last sonnet addressed to the ladies of Lyons, qual-
ifies the overwhelming power ascribed to love. The vivid
expression that she allows it in the preceding sonnets indicates,
however, a conscious indulgence in its insubstantial pleasures, not
the least of which are the joys of writing about them.

From the objective point of view of the scholastic theology
which prevailed in the Middle Ages, love was a symptom of the
poverty of humanity. The emotional turmoil of the individual
counted for little in the all-encompassing structure of Thomist
Aristotelianism. Any suffering simply proved his lack of worth.
The new status of the poet, as it developed in the Renaissance,
announced an upgraded value for the poet's work, no matter what
his or her subject. Paradoxically, though, this mythical status
tended to distance the poet from a negative interpretation of
human misery in love, which Petrarch had seen as an indication of
man's fallen state. Shakespeare's sonnets brilliantly portray the
polarities of the human condition. On the one hand, they are
pervaded by melancholy. Awareness of the encroachment of age,
of the limitations of the finite, of the corruption of the power
structure of society, of the ultimate futility of human endeavour,
are all basic features of these poems. Yet, the upward swing engendered by the inspiration of the beautiful young man, to whom
Shakespeare addressed so many of his early sonnets, enables the
mind to take flight. A poet and lover, impelled by passion, can read
beyond the cruel strictures of life and find a pattern which speaks
of an alternative logic, one that differs from the arid, reductive
objectivity of scholastic theology. The alternative logic found in
this way is a truth of its kind. It is one coined by a deprived
humanity, driven to look beyond the immediate for some other
meaningful dimension to life. Chekhov's story 'The Black Monk'

illustrates the necessity for this impulse to give life an impetus which encourages a human being to engage positively with others. When, in Chekhov's story, Anton is 'cured' of the imaginary visits from the monk, who continually assured him of his worth, he becomes negative and surly. He loses his lust for life. For Shakespeare, such galvanising of positive responses to life and a deep sense of its worth provide in themselves the substance of much of his verse. The validity of the 'marriage of true minds', described passionately in all its unlikeliness, is asserted as an act of faith:

> If this be false or 'pon me proved
> I never writ, nor no man ever loved.

Writing and loving are both projects which suspend slavery to the immediate deficiencies of humanity. They are the forces which are aroused by the beautiful young man.

Shakespeare drew with care from the myth presented in the *Phaedrus* to construct his poetic identity as an inspired lover, in a quest for essential truth. He is thus able to present in the collection a search for a truth which transcends the imminent. Some sonnets do indeed present a melancholy perception of life unadorned. These sonnets, in all their scepticism, offer a bleak contrast to the delirious inspiration provided by the figure of the young man. However, although there is a fundamental difference in these perspectives, they are not totally irreconcilable. Those sonnets placed at the beginning of the collection recurrently implore the young man to have a child. This plea would appear to indicate a positive feature in the moral landscape of Shakespeare's sonnets: the ability to have a child links humanity with the mystery of divine creation. Whether or not Shakespeare remained a Catholic has been much discussed. The sonnets rarely draw on a lexis of Christian faith. However, the emphasis on the value of child bearing in the early sonnets indicates a basically positive outlook. The love inspired by beautiful youth is a refined love; it is not contaminated like the lust described in Sonnet 129. The love described for the youth is a basic element in a transcendent perception of the universe in which truth is angled from the view of the lover, a view which is presented here as privileged. The wide-ranging compass of the sonnets suggests moreover that the complex substance of the self has both need and resources to transcend the shackles of its blighted condition.

By contrast, John Donne's rigorous Anglican faith acted as a stern reminder of his intrinsic limitations. His apostasy caused the negative doctrine of the Reformation to be so ingrained into his thinking that he saw the self as the source of sin. Donne's love poetry, when understood in this light, shows indulgence in love as an example of the distortion of truth brought about by human egoism. Often, Donne's verse is satiric, making of love the basis of a joke at man's expense. This poem (from *Songs and sonnets*), 'The Paradox', pinpoints the essential contradictions in the lover's outlook:

> No lover saith, I love, nor any other
> Can judge a perfect lover;
> He thinks that else none can, nor will agree
> That any loves but he:
> I cannot say I loved, for who can say
> He was killed yesterday?
> Love with excess of heat more young than old,

Death kills with too much cold;
We die but once, and who loved last did die,
He that saith twice, doth lie:
For though he seem to move, and stir awhile,
It doth the sense beguile.
Such life is like the light which bideth yet
When the light's life is set,
Or like the heat, which fire in solid matter
Leaves behind, two hours after.
Once I loved and died; and am now become
Mine epitaph and tomb.
Here dead men speak their last, and so do I;
Love-slain, lo, here I lie.

There is an almost bitter satiric tone in this and similar ironic poems, emphasising Donne's contempt for the delusions propagated by self-indulgent, self-centred humanity. And yet much of his love poetry is tender, for all its recognition of love as the epitome of human weakness. Personal experience creates this additional dimension. The poems Donne wrote at his wife's death are steeped in the misery which this loss caused him. 'The Nocturnal upon St Lucy's Day' shows how the death of the woman he loved has robbed him of his essential being, an indication of the insubstantial and perilous nature of the human sense of identity. Without the solace of her life, her lover has no sense of his existence:

But I am by her death (which word wrongs her)
Of the first nothing, the Elixir grown;
Were I a man, that I were one,
I needs must know; I should prefer,

If I were any beast,
Some ends, some means; Yea plants, yea stones detest
And love; All, all some properties invest;
If I an ordinary nothing were,
As shadow, a light, and body must be here.
But I am none; nor will my Sun renew. (28-37)

Donne here seems to make a conceit of the very concept of existence. He presents his awareness as only possible in terms of the life of the beloved. As a poet, he suggests that the very existence of plants and stones demonstrates that they too must be infused with emotional responses. The death of his beloved has reduced him to a non-entity.

This poem, and also the Holy Sonnet XVII in which he laments the death of his wife, show how the devastation of her loss is essentially salutary, since through it he is brought to recognise his need of God. In Sonnet XVII the two loves of his life are brought together: he weighs that for his wife against that for God, and finds his love for her to be but a stage in finding God's love:

Here the admiring her my mind did whet
To seek thee God; so streams do show their head;
But though I have found thee, and thou my thirst has fed,
A holy thirsty dropsy melt me yet.
But why should I beg more love, when as thou
Dost woo my soul, for hers offering all thine; (5-10)

Donne's love poetry involves a dialogue with himself. He rejected his early poetry for its basis in fallacy. Yet the maturity of his Holy Sonnets, which express his need of God's love, is based on the self-knowledge which so ravaged him.

I have called the treatment of love in Racine's drama the 'high noon' of self-awareness. This is because its theatricality is in some way reductive. The passionate self is dramatised by Racine to exemplify an implacable force in human response. As such, its dramatic potential is both moving and terrifying. Yet its component parts are drawn from a cultural legacy, and the result is designed to entertain a specific audience. There is no personal creative struggle, born of the dreams and despair of an individual life. In its adjustment to the formation and tastes of its audience, Racine's drama is very like the songs of the troubadours. The distress he imparts through performance of his characters is doomed by the very context of its creation. As a result, the audience is given the thrill of the onlooker, but not the inner intimacy of the silent reader.

At its most creative, and disturbing, the idiom of love is the idiom of life. Writer and reader meet in the intimacy of an encounter with the several dimensions of their existence.

Bibliography

Augustine, St, *The City of God*, 2 vols., Everyman Library, London, 1967.

Bradshaw, Graham, *Shakespeare's Scepticism*, New York, 1987.

Carey, John, Donne: *Life Mind and Art*, London, 1981.

Donne, John, A Critical Edition of Major Works, ed. Carey, Oxford, 1990.

Du Bellay, Joachim, *La Deffence et illustration de la langue fracoyse*, ed. Chamard, Paris, 1948.

Erasmus, Desiderius, *Praise of Folly and letter to Martin Dorp*, ed. Levi, Harmondsworth, 1963.

Hammond, Nicholas, *Creative Tensions: An Introduction to Seventeenth-Century Literature*, London, 1997.

Labé, Louise, *Oeuvres complètes*, ed. Rigolot, Paris, 1986.

Lewis, C.S., *The Allegory of Love*, Oxford, 1958.

Minta, Stephen, *Petrarch and Petrarchism: The English and French Traditions*, Manchester, 1980.

Oppenheimer, Paul, *The Birth of the Modern Mind*, Oxford, 1989.

Petrarch, Francesco, *The Canzoniere* or rerum *vulgarium fragmenta*, ed. And transl. Musa, Indiana, 1996.

Plato, *Phaedrus and letters V11 and V111*, trans. Cohen, London, 1973.

Rabelais, François, *Gargantua and Pantagruel*, Harmondsworth, 1963.

Racine, Jean, *Phèdre*, London, 1996.

Shakespeare, *William, the Sonnets and A Lover's Complaint*, 1986.

Vvyan, John, *Shakespeare and Platonic Beauty*, London 1961.

Walton, Izaak, *The Lives of John Donne*, London 1973.

Yeats, W.B. *Collected Poems*, 1961.

Index